To : Dad
From : Jason
Because you're 74

MW00454662

What Is Saving Faith?

Other books by John Piper

What Is Saving Faith?

Reflections on Receiving Christ as a Treasure

John Piper

 CROSSWAY®

WHEATON, ILLINOIS

Hardcover ISBN: 978-1-4335-7836-6
ePub ISBN: 978-1-4335-7839-7
PDF ISBN: 978-1-4335-7837-3
Mobipocket ISBN: 978-1-4335-7838-0

Library of Congress Cataloging-in-Publication Data

Names: Piper, John, 1946– author.
Title: What is saving faith? : reflections on receiving Christ as a treasure / John Piper.
Description: Wheaton, Ilinois : Crossway, 2022. | Includes bibliographical references and index.
Identifiers: LCCN 2021025373 (print) | LCCN 2021025374 (ebook) | ISBN 9781433578366 (hardcover) | ISBN 9781433578373 (pdf) | ISBN 9781433578380 (mobi) | ISBN 9781433578397 (epub) Subjects: LCSH: Salvation—Christianity. | Faith. | Experience (Religion)
Classification: LCC BT751.3 .P58 2022 (print) | LCC BT751.3 (ebook) | DDC 234—dc23
LC record available at https://lccn.loc.gov/2021025373
LC ebook record available at https://lccn.loc.gov/2021025374

Crossway is a publishing ministry of Good News Publishers.

VP   31   30   29   28   27   26   25   24   23   22
15   14   13   12   11   10   9   8   7   6   5   4   3   2   1

For David and Karin Livingston
incomparable friends
in the joys of treasuring Christ

I could not love Thee, so blind and unfeeling;
Covenant promises fell not to me.
Then without warning, desire, or deserving,
I found my treasure, my pleasure, in Thee.

I have no merit to woo or delight Thee,
I have no wisdom or pow'rs to employ;
Yet in Thy mercy, how pleasing Thou find'st me,
This is Thy pleasure: that Thou art my joy.

Contents

Introduction

What Are We Really Asking?

WHY DO SO MANY thoughtful Christians from centuries ago describe saving faith as though it were an experience involving the affections and not just a decision of the will? Why does John Calvin refer to saving faith as a "warm embrace" and "pious affection"?[1] Why does Henry Scougal call it a "feeling persuasion of spiritual things"?[2] Why does Peter van Mastricht call it a "reception with delight"?[3] And why does Jonathan Edwards say, "Love is the main thing in saving faith"?[4]

---

1 See, respectively, John Calvin, *Commentaries of the Epistles of Paul to the Galatians and Ephesians*, trans. William Pringle (Bellingham, WA: Logos Bible Software, 2010), 262; and John Calvin, *Institutes of the Christian Religion*, trans. Henry Beveridge, 2 vols. (Edinburgh: Calvin Translation Society, 1845), 3.2.8.

2 Henry Scougal, *The Life of God in the Soul of Man* (Fearn, Ross-Shire, UK: Christian Focus, 2001), 53.

3 Petrus van Mastricht, *Faith in the Triune God*, ed. Joel R. Beeke, trans. Todd M. Rester and Michael T. Spangler, vol. 2, Theoretical-Practical Theology (Grand Rapids, MI: Reformation Heritage, 2019), 9.

4 Jonathan Edwards, *Writings on the Trinity, Grace, and Faith*, ed. Sang Hyun Lee and Harry S. Stout, vol. 21, *The Works of Jonathan Edwards* (New Haven, CT: Yale University Press, 2003), 448. This is one of the most controversial statements we will wrestle with. But let's make sure we are wrestling throughout the book with what Edwards

My perception is that millions of people who say they have saving faith would hear these voices as though they were a foreign language. Maybe the mature, older saints arrive at such a lofty notion of faith. But that's not how salvation happens. That's not *saving* faith. That's something else. Saving faith is a decision to accept Christ as Savior. Or if you're really serious, as Savior *and* Lord. It's not about affections but about volitions. "*Choose* this day whom you will serve" (Josh. 24:15). Such might be the response of many Christians. I think that response, including the notion of saving faith behind it, is deficient and, for many, deadly.

What then is saving faith—and not just theoretically but in our real-life experience? The question is a burning one. It is urgent and serious and personal—do I have saving faith? Am I saved? "By grace you have been saved *through faith*" (Eph. 2:8). "Whoever *believes* has eternal life" (John 6:47). Does that include me? Do I have *saving faith*?

Is Faith Really an Experience?

I am asking about the *experience* of saving faith—what are the conscious dynamics of it? What is it like in the head—the reason? What is it like in the heart—the affections? What is it like to experience it?

Even the very word *experience* is a stumbling block to some, since they see the word *experience* as connoting mystical or emotional

---

really means. When Edwards speaks of *love* in this sentence, he does not mean love for people, but rather love for God. Nor is he thinking of love for God as obedience to God's commandments. Nor is he thinking of love as a "giving grace." If you lay on Edwards a sentence like, "Faith is a receiving grace, whereas love is a giving grace," you will misconstrue Edwards. *Love* in this sentence is profoundly a "receiving grace"—receiving God himself as supremely precious. Throughout this book, that is the way I will use the word *love* whenever love is contemplated as part of saving faith. See especially chaps. 18 and 19.

highs and lows, which they want to distinguish from faith entirely. For example, J. I. Packer wrote, "Faith is a relationship of recognition, credence, and trust and is not in itself an experience."[5] I'll admit that I don't like that sentence, though J. I. Packer is one of my heroes![6] I doubt we would have had a substantive difference if we clarified the word *experience*.

When I use the word *experience*, I don't have in mind any particular intensity of emotion, or any particular height of mental clarity, or any mystical occurrence. All I imply by the word *experience* is that faith happens in us, and when it does, it is a conscious event, and we are involved with it. And I mean *morally* involved—not the way we are involved with a sneeze or a headache. *Experience*, as I am using the word in relation to faith, is not an amoral sensation that sweeps over us like shivers in the cold. It is something taking place in the mind and will. The thinking of the mind and the inclining of the will are involved. Perceiving and approving or disapproving are part of the experience I am talking about.[7]

I want to know what the Bible reveals to us about the experience of faith. What is its nature? Faith is not a theory. It is not an idea. It is *experienced* in the mind and heart, or we are not saved. That is important.

What Does *Affectional* Mean?

Specifically, I want to know if there is in the very nature of saving faith some kind of *affectional* element. That is, does saving faith include any element of love for Christ, or admiration, or adoration,

---

5   J. I. Packer, *Knowing Christianity* (Downers Grove, IL: InterVarsity Press, 1999), 6.

6   See my tribute to Dr. Packer, who died on July 17, 2020: "Reformation Theology in the Hands of a Servant," July 18, 2020, Desiring God website, https://desiringgod.org/.

7   For more reflections on faith as an experience that is different from a decision, see chap. 25, pp. 251–53.

or treasuring, or cherishing, or delighting, or satisfaction, or thankfulness, or revering? All these words are affectional. They represent experiences in the human soul that I am calling *affections*. And I will argue in this book that saving faith does indeed have in its very nature affectional elements, dimensions, or aspects.

When I use the term *affections* or *affectional*, I don't have in view any physical acts of the body, or even *natural* acts of the mind or heart. I *do* have in mind experiences of the heart that go beyond mental awareness, or cognition, or persuasion, or conviction, or resolve, or decision. None of those words is by itself affectional. When I describe saving faith in this book as affectional, I am not referring to something merely natural. I am referring to *spiritual* affections, not natural ones.

Natural emotions are not spiritual affections. But spiritual affections are a spiritual form of emotion. That is, the heart is moved. Some kind of *feeling* happens that goes beyond thoughts or ideas or decisions. But it is not a merely *natural* feeling. It is the kind of thing that caused Henry Scougal to use the phrase "*feeling persuasion* of spiritual things."[8]

When I use the term *affectional* or *affections*, I am thinking of them as the special work of the Holy Spirit. I am thinking in the terms of 1 Corinthians 2:14: "The *natural* person does not accept the things of the Spirit of God, for they are folly to him, and he is not able to understand them because they are *spiritually* discerned." In other words, the love, delight, and satisfaction I am asking about are not merely *natural human experiences*. They are divine gifts. They are the work of the Spirit. But they are no less experiences, and no less affections, because of that.

8 See introduction note 2.

I don't say this to prejudge my findings, but simply to clarify terminology. I am happy for the Bible to correct me if my terminology proves ill-advised. But I am eager to avoid ambiguity and confusion around terminology. And I know that the noun *affections* and the adjective *affectional* can be easily misunderstood.

The Question Is Not about the *Fruit* of Spiritual Affections

To be even more precise, I am not asking whether affections like *love* for Christ,[9] or *delight* in his glory, or *satisfaction* in his perfections, or *treasuring* his worth *accompany* saving faith. I am not asking if such affections are the *result* of saving faith. I am asking whether such affectional realities are in the very exercise of faith itself. That is, are they part of the nature of faith? Are any of these affections so *integral* to saving faith that, if they were not there, we would not have saving faith? And I will try to show from the Bible that the answer to this question is yes. Saving faith has affectional elements without which the faith is not saving.

Therefore, it is not enough for me to show that certain spiritual affections are necessary for *final* salvation. It is true that there are spiritual affections that are the inevitable *fruit* and *confirmation* of authentic faith. For example, there is no doubt in my mind that love to Christ is absolutely necessary for final salvation. I could point to Jesus's words, "Whoever loves son or daughter more than me is not worthy of me" (Matt. 10:37), or to Paul's words, "If anyone has no love for the Lord, let him be accursed" (1 Cor. 16:22). These,

---

9   It will become clear in chaps. 18 and 19 that (1) I am not using the term *love* in contexts like this to refer to our active obedience to Christ (see introduction note 4), and (2) I am not treating the heart's love to Christ as identical to saving faith. Saving faith is always more than its affectional elements. The question is, as the next sentence stresses, Is there any dimension of the heart's love for Christ that the Bible treats as integral to saving faith?

and many others, show that such spiritual affections are necessary for *final* salvation.

But are they necessary because they are the *result* and *confirmation* of saving faith, or are they necessary because they are *part* of saving faith? Showing that these affections are necessary for final salvation is important. But that is not my main concern. I want to know if any spiritual affections are *integral* to saving faith, not just its effects. Which calls for another clarification.

Is *Faith* Saving, or Is *Christ* Saving?

When I speak of *saving* faith, I do not mean to imply that faith somehow has usurped the place of Jesus Christ as the one who saves. "Christ Jesus came into the world to save sinners" (1 Tim. 1:15). Christ the Lord is our Savior. "Unto you is born this day in the city of David a Savior, who is Christ the Lord" (Luke 2:11). Faith is never called our Savior.

Nevertheless, Jesus said to more than one person, "Your faith has saved you" (ἡ πίστις σου σέσωκέν σε, Matt. 9:22; Mark 5:34; 10:52; Luke 7:50; 8:48; 17:19; 18:42). Even though this is usually translated, "Your faith has *healed* you" or "Your faith has *made* you *well*," the point stands: *Jesus* is the healer, yet he says that *faith* healed. He means that faith was the human instrument through which he himself healed. That's what I mean when I say that faith saves. I mean Jesus saves, and faith is the Spirit-given human instrument through which he does it.

So, to use more traditional theological terms, faith is the *instrumental* cause (not the *ground*) of our justification. Christ—including his blood and righteousness—is the *ground*. Faith is the receiving *instrument*. Allowing for imperfect analogies, faith saves the way swallowing a pill heals. But the pill (not the swallowing) contains the disease-killing agent, the health-giving power. Faith receives Christ. Christ saves. In that sense, faith saves.

You might say I am asking the question in James 2:14: "Can that faith save him?" James meant, Can faith that does not produce good works save a person (James 2:26)? But I am not asking whether faith that does not produce *good works* can save; rather, I'm asking whether faith that does not include affectional elements, such as *treasuring* Jesus, can save.

Inadequacy of Isolated Words

For a long time, I have been troubled by the inadequacy of the words *faith* and *belief* and *trust* (or any other single words) to make clear what is required in order to be saved. One might object, "But those are the very words that Scripture uses to describe how to be saved. '*Believe* in the Lord Jesus, and you will be saved' (Acts 16:31). Are you saying that God doesn't know how best to communicate the way of salvation?"

No, I am not saying that. I am saying that in the Scriptures these words are not isolated. They are bricks embedded in the beautiful building of God-inspired truth. Words by themselves cannot carry the reality they are intended to carry unless we see the design that the skillful brick masons were creating when they put the bricks together the way they did. Or to say it more prosaically, we will not know what *faith* and *belief* and *trust* mean unless we press into the way they are used in the most illuminating biblical contexts.

Even our own experience impels us to probe into those contexts for more depth and precision. Experience teaches us to probe for distinctions. We know there are different kinds of faith and different ways of trusting. For example, experience teaches us that it is possible, even necessary at times, to *trust* a person with our lives whom we neither love, nor admire, nor even want to be around. Which of these two would we *trust* for our brain surgery: a foul-mouthed, dishonest, lustful, highly skilled, highly effective surgeon at the top of his profession, or a kind, honest, chaste young surgeon with little actual experience? We would trust the lecher with our life. Which means what?

Something Has Been Assumed

The traditional way of describing saving faith has always *assumed* something. For centuries, theologians have *assumed* that saving faith includes more than the confidence that Christ is competent, like the lecherous surgeon. When the three traditional descriptions of faith were used, there was an assumption that the word *fiducia* (cordial trust) alongside *notitia* (knowledge) and *assensus* (mental assent) included *more* than trusting Jesus as an ignominious but effective rescuer from hell. None of those who used the word *fiducia* (trust) to describe the heart of saving faith intended a kind of trust that views Jesus as disliked, unadmirable, undesired, distasteful, repugnant. They would have said, "Saving faith does not experience Christ that way."

Theologians and pastors and thoughtful laypeople have always known that the isolated words *faith* and *believe* contain ambiguities that need clarification. And they have endeavored to see these words embedded in the biblical texts designed by God to clarify and fill up their meaning. I will try to show from some of these texts (the book is not exhaustive) that part of that fullness is the affectional dimension of saving faith.

Treasuring Is Not Just One Thing

I use the term *treasuring Christ* as my default summary expression of the affectional nature of saving faith. I take the verb *treasure* to be a fitting experiential counterpart to the noun *treasure*. I will argue that Christ is the essence of the treasure in texts like Matthew 13:44, "The kingdom of heaven is like *treasure* hidden in a field"; and 2 Corinthians 4:7, "We have this *treasure* in jars of clay."

When I say that *treasuring Christ* is my *summary* expression of the affectional nature of saving faith, I mean to imply that there are diverse affections in the nature of saving faith, not just one. The heart experiences treasuring Christ differently as it embraces different aspects of Christ's greatness and beauty and worth.

There is joyful treasuring, because we taste the substance of the joy set before us (Heb. 11:1; 12:2). There is treasuring like the satisfying of hunger, because Christ is the bread of life (John 6:35, 51). There is treasuring like the pleasure of quenched thirst, because Christ is the fountain of living water (John 4:10–11). There is treasuring like the love of light after darkness, because Christ is the radiance of divine glory (John 1:14; 3:19). There is treasuring like the love of truth, because Christ in the gospel is the preciousness of true reality (2 Thess. 2:10–12). And this list could be extended as far as there are glories of Christ to be known. Saving faith treasures them all, as each is known. All are precious. All are treasured. But the affectional experience is not the same in each case. So it is in the way Christ is received by saving faith.

Christ Treasured in All His Excellencies

Perhaps I should clarify an important implication lest I be misunderstood in speaking of Jesus as our treasure. In calling Jesus a treasure, I do not mean that he is a treasure *alongside* other roles or excellencies. I mean that he is a treasure *in* all his roles and excellencies. We may speak loosely about receiving Christ as Lord and Savior and treasure. I regularly use that way of speaking. But

I do not mean that his worth is like a third role he plays alongside Lord and Savior.

Rather, when we focus on Jesus as our treasure, we include *all* that he is: treasured Savior, treasured Lord, treasured wisdom, treasured righteousness, treasured friend, treasured living water, treasured bread of heaven, and more. Christ as a treasure is not a slice of Christ. It is every dimension of Christ—all of Christ—making up the totality of his infinite value.

I will argue in this book that saving faith has in it the affectional dimension of treasuring Christ. Where Christ is not received as treasure, he is being used. This is not saving faith. It is tragic that many think it is.

Supreme Treasure?

Sometimes in this book, I will speak of saving faith as receiving Christ as our *supreme* treasure. Other times, I will refer simply to receiving Christ as our treasure. I mean no distinction. Saving faith always views Christ as having supreme value. That is how he is received. To embrace Christ as a second- or third-tier treasure is not saving faith. It is an affront.

Jesus told a story to illustrate how it offends him when we fail to treasure him above the things of this world:

> A man once gave a great banquet and invited many. And at the time for the banquet he sent his servant to say to those who had been invited, "Come, for everything is now ready." But they all alike began to make excuses. The first said to him, "I have bought a field, and I must go out and see it. Please have me excused." And another said, "I have bought five yoke of oxen, and I go to examine them. Please have me excused." And another said,

"I have married a wife, and therefore I cannot come." So the servant came and reported these things to his master. Then the master of the house became angry. (Luke 14:16–21)

Real estate. Possessions. Family. To prefer these over the treasure of Christ makes him angry. It is an affront to him and destruction to us. Of course, the story doesn't end there. It gets better and worse.

The anger of the host is transposed into the compassion of the Great Commission. If my people will not treasure what I offer, "Go out quickly to the streets and lanes of the city, and bring in the poor and crippled and blind and lame. . . . Go out to the highways and hedges and compel people to come in, that my house may be filled" (Luke 14:21, 23). But for those who would not treasure the Master, judgment falls: "I tell you, none of those men who were invited shall taste my banquet" (Luke 14:24).

Saving faith receives Christ as a treasure, but not as second to lands, oxen, or spouses. He is valued above them. Or he is rejected. Embracing him as one among many useful treasures is worse than useless. It is worse because it gives the impression that he is willing to be used. He is not. He will be received as our supreme treasure, or not at all. "Whoever loves father or mother more than me is not worthy of me" (Matt. 10:37). "Any one of you who does not renounce all that he has cannot be my disciple" (Luke 14:33). "I count everything as loss because of the surpassing worth of knowing Christ Jesus my Lord" (Phil. 3:8). This book is an argument that such texts are describing dimensions of saving faith.

How the Book Flows

After the introduction, part 1 of the book addresses six roots from which my concern has grown. What experiences and controversies and questions in my life have aroused in me the commitment to clarify the nature of saving faith? Then I devote part 2 to defining saving faith from the New Testament in a broad, general sense.

I move toward the heart of the matter in part 3, asking whether saving faith is indeed a receiving of Christ as our supreme treasure. Part 4 is the book's climax as the question of part 3 is sharpened: Does receiving Christ as our treasure mean that saving faith does indeed include affectional elements that may be summed up as treasuring Christ? Does receiving Christ as a treasure mean treasuring Christ?

Finally, in part 5 I deal with implications for evangelism and for the assurance of salvation. If saving faith includes treasuring Christ above all things, how does that affect the way we call people to faith? And how does it affect the way we ourselves "show the same earnestness to have the full assurance of hope until the end" (Heb. 6:11)?

In the conclusion, I relate the main point of the book to my lifelong effort to clarify and commend Christian Hedonism,[10] and to the ultimate purpose of God to be glorified in a redeemed people who are satisfied in him.

I pray that if God leads you to read on, you will "test everything; [and] hold fast what is good" (1 Thess. 5:21).[11] I think that

---

10 An introduction to what I mean by Christian Hedonism can be read or watched at the Desiring God website, "What Is Christian Hedonism?," August 1, 2015, https://www.desiring god.org/. The foundational book in which I put forth Christian Hedonism is *Desiring God: Meditations of a Christian Hedonist* (Colorado Springs, CO: Multnomah, 2011).

11 As part of my own "testing all things," I sent a draft of this book for feedback to a number of respected brothers with high-level experience and biblical wisdom and academic rigor. Eight of them wrote significant responses. I added numerous clarifications because of their helpful input. Some were concerned that what I am saying may obscure or even contradict the precious doctrine of justification by faith alone. My hope is that chaps. 3

means test it all by the Scriptures. I make no claim to have any authority in myself. I believe the Scriptures are the word of God and therefore true. They communicate reality. I have tried to be faithful to them. May the Lord lavish his grace upon you in all wisdom and insight (Eph. 1:8).

---

and 4 remove that concern. But in case a more direct response might help, I have added an appendix as a brief response and challenge.

PART 1

THE ROOTS OF
MY CONCERN

More powerful than all the other forces that pressed me to write this book is the lifelong habit of reading the Bible every day. Chapters 1 through 6 will describe the theological battles, cultural pressures, historical inspirations, and contemporary challenges that motivated me. But nothing in these chapters comes close to the simple fact that reading the Bible has filled me with a longing to know what God brings about in his children when he gives them saving faith. I want to understand what my mind and heart are doing when I believe in Christ.

Yes, this implies that we can experience the wonders of saving faith without a clear and full grasp of what saving faith is. You don't have to be a theologian to be a Christian. If the only thing we could experience is what we could explain, no one could become a

Christian. Conversion is a God-given miracle. With it, saving faith comes into being. We will spend eternity discovering the wonders of the experience of saving faith.

So year after year of reading the Bible, the questions pile up. There are always more questions than answers. To be sure, there are many answers. Spectacular answers. All the answers we need to glorify God and do his will. But every day, there are new questions:

- Jesus, if you say that you are the supreme treasure (Matt. 13:44), and that receiving you is what faith does (John 1:12), then what is it like when faith receives you as such a treasure?

- When you describe believing as coming to you to drink and never thirsting again (John 6:35), what are you saying about faith and the soul's satisfaction?

- Paul, what do you mean when you say that we can have faith—even mountain-moving faith—and still come to nothing in our lives (1 Cor. 13:2)?

- What do you mean, Paul, when you say that we can believe the gospel "in vain" (1 Cor. 15:2)?

- Why do you contrast "not believ[ing] the truth" with having "pleasure in unrighteousness" (2 Thess. 2:12)?

- If the gift of faith is the new ability to see the glory of Christ (2 Cor. 4:6), and if there are "eyes" in our hearts (Eph. 1:18), then why do you say that we walk by faith and not by sight (2 Cor. 5:7)?

- How is it that faith has the amazing power to cause people to love each other (Gal. 5:6; 1 Tim. 1:5), and that everything that does not come from faith is sin (Rom. 14:23)? What is it about faith that makes loving people inevitable?

- Since you say that Abraham grew strong in his faith, giving glory to God (Rom. 4:20), would I be justified in saying that God is not glorified by being trusted for a promise while being regarded as embarrassing and boring?

- And, John, how does faith overcome the world and turn burdensome commandments into happy obedience (1 John 5:3–4)?

- Finally, whoever you are who wrote the great, Christ-exalting book of Hebrews, what am I to make of your definition of saving faith as "the substance of things hoped for" (Heb. 11:1 KJV)? Or should I not translate ὑπόστασις (*hupostasis*) as "substance" like the old-timers, but as "assurance"?

I just used the word *finally*. But only because ten questions is enough to give you the flavor of where this book came from. It came from a lifetime of reading the Bible with the habit of asking questions.

Of course, we don't write books about every question. God has his ways to make some questions rise to the point of producing a book. That divine action does not happen in a vacuum. Which brings us back to the theological battles, cultural pressures, historical inspirations, and contemporary challenges that have urged on and shaped this book. That is what we turn to now.

1

Taking the Lordship Battle to Another Level

THE LONGER I LIVE, and the closer I come to heaven, the more troubling it is that so many people identify as Christians but give so little evidence of being truly Christian. The more I ponder the radical, miraculous nature of the new birth,[1] and its absolute necessity for entering the kingdom of God (John 3:3, 5), the more distressing it is how many professing Christians seem so cavalier about being new creatures in Christ.

"I Never Knew You"

My sadness grows when I consider that there may be millions of people who think of themselves as heaven-bound, hell-escaping Christians who are not—people for whom Christ is at the margins of their thoughts and affections, not at the transforming center.

---

1 Of course, the "new birth" is part of a larger miraculous work of God in saving us, stretching from election in eternity past (Eph. 1:4) to glorification at the resurrection (Rom. 8:30; Phil. 3:21) and into eternity future. For a fuller treatment of the new birth, see John Piper, *Finally Alive: What Happens When We Are Born Again* (Fearn, Ross-Shire, UK: Christian Focus, 2009).

People who will hear Jesus say at the judgment, "I never knew you; depart from me" (Matt. 7:23).

As I have pondered the roots of this looming calamity, I have not been able to escape the conviction that it is partly rooted in a widespread misunderstanding about what saving faith is—not just among nominal Christians, but also among pastors who don't show the unsuspecting "Christians" their error. Of course, I am not the only one who has seen this impending shock coming for nominal Christians at the judgment of Christ. Many have sounded the alarm about this deadly disease of churchgoing unbelief, even if their diagnosis of the cause is not exactly the one I am dealing with in this book.

MacArthur's Timely Blast across the Bow

For example, in the first decade of my pastoral ministry, the 1980s, this issue took the form of the controversy over so-called "lordship salvation." Do we need to submit to Jesus as Lord as well as believe on him as Savior in order to be saved? The most important and biblically wise book published in that skirmish may have been John MacArthur's *The Gospel according to Jesus* (1988).[2]

The book was a response to the very crisis of Christian nominalism that I just expressed. MacArthur asks, "Who knows how many people are deluded into believing they are saved when they are not?"[3] When the book was published, I read it like a miser finding gold. I wrote, "As for my own personal response to the book, I could scarcely put it down for joy."[4] To give you a glimpse into

---

2   John MacArthur, *The Gospel according to Jesus* (Grand Rapids, MI: Zondervan, 1988).

3   MacArthur, *Gospel according to Jesus*, 79.

4   John Piper, "Putting God Back into Faith: Review of *The Gospel according to Jesus*, by John MacArthur," February 1989, Desiring God website, https://www.desiringgod.org/.

the controversy, here are the beginning paragraphs of my laudatory response to MacArthur's book from those days:

When latter-day Puritans J. I. Packer and James Boice both write enthusiastic forewords for a confessed "premillennial dispensationalist" (25), the common adversary must be ominous. What alarm welded this unusual coalition? Answer:

> "Loud voices from the dispensationalist camp are putting forth the teaching that it is possible to reject Christ as Lord yet receive Him as Savior" (27). One such voice says, "It is possible, but miserable, to be saved without ever making Christ Lord of your life" (204).

Lewis Sperry Chafer wrote, "The New Testament does not impose repentance upon the unsaved as a condition of salvation" (161). *The Ryrie Study Bible* calls repentance a "false addition to faith" when made a condition of salvation (161).

So [in this view] there is no necessary connection between saving faith and obedience. Faith is essentially a momentary mental assent to gospel facts (170). Fruit is not a legitimate test of faith's authenticity.

The resulting mass of disobedient nominal Christians are accommodated under the category of mere "believer" over against the category of "disciple," which refers to the stage-two Christian who "makes Jesus Lord" of his life (30). Zane Hodges says, "How fortunate that one's entrance into the kingdom of God [does] not depend on his discipleship" (196).[5]

---

5 Piper, "Putting God Back into Faith." See below pp. 241–49 for my understanding of repentance in relation to saving faith. Page numbers cited are from MacArthur, *The Gospel according to Jesus.*

Wayne Grudem's *Free Grace*

Lest we think the view that MacArthur was challenging has gone away, we should take notice that Wayne Grudem, in 2016, thirty years after that dispute, felt so burdened by its encroachments in evangelical churches today that he published a new book, *"Free Grace" Theology: 5 Ways It Diminishes the Gospel.*[6] Both Grudem and MacArthur faithfully show from Scripture, in the words of MacArthur: "The signature of saving faith is surrender to the lordship of Jesus Christ." "Those who refuse Him as Lord cannot use Him as Savior."[7] "Faith obeys. Unbelief rebels. The fruit of one's life reveals whether that person is a believer or an unbeliever."[8]

My Different Question

Here's the difference between the book you are now reading and those books. Neither MacArthur nor Grudem probed the question I am posing: Does the very nature of saving faith include a treasuring of Christ as supremely valuable—that is, an affectional dimension that may hold the key to why saving faith necessarily severs the root of sin and bears the fruit of glad obedience? I don't intend this as a criticism of MacArthur or Grudem. They both stand firmly (as I do) in the Reformed teaching of the Westminster Confession, chapter 11, section 2:

> Faith, thus receiving and resting on Christ and his righteousness is the sole instrument of justification; *yet it is not alone in*

6 Wayne Grudem, *"Free Grace" Theology: 5 Ways It Diminishes the Gospel* (Wheaton, IL: Crossway, 2016).

7 MacArthur, *The Gospel according to Jesus*, 209, 10.

8 MacArthur, *The Gospel according to Jesus*, 178.

the person justified, but is ever accompanied with all other saving graces, and is no dead faith, but works by love. (emphasis added)

In other words, we agree that the only faith that justifies is the kind of faith that works by love—the love that Paul says is summed up in "Love your neighbor as yourself" (Gal. 5:14; see also 5:6).[9] This is what both MacArthur and Grudem stress: faith is not saving faith if it is not the sort that "works by love." That is, Christ is not a sin-covering Savior where he is not embraced as a love-creating Lord.

But neither MacArthur nor Grudem focuses on *why* saving faith necessarily produces holy conduct. Or more precisely, they do not focus on the question, What is it about the nature of saving faith that is so transformative? That question is part of what is driving this book. Specifically, does saving faith include in it, by God's grace, a kind of *affectional embrace of Christ* that gives it the transformative force that it clearly has in the Bible? And is that affectional embrace the receiving of Christ as our supreme treasure?

Taking *Future Grace* Even Deeper

The answer to those questions took shape in my mind over the next five years, after the peak of the lordship controversy. In 1995, I published *The Purifying Power of Living by Faith in Future Grace.*[10] This was my effort to deal with the same issue that MacArthur and Grudem dealt with, only with a focus on *how* saving faith necessarily produces holiness of life. I argued that at the heart of saving faith is a deep, affectional dimension—a Spirit-given, Spirit-sustained

9   On my understanding of Gal. 5:6, see pp. 124–25 and chapter 11.
10 John Piper, *The Purifying Power of Living by Faith in Future Grace* (Sisters, OR: Multnomah, 1995). The revised edition was published under the title *Future Grace: The Purifying Power of the Promises of God* (Colorado Springs, CO: Multnomah, 2012).

satisfaction in all that God is for us in Jesus, including all that God *promises to be* for us in Christ. This satisfaction in Christ is not merely a *result* of saving faith but part of what it *is*.[11] The book attempted to show how that experience of saving faith breaks the power of sin and empowers love for our neighbor.

Now I am returning, in the present book, to provide a more exegetically thorough foundation for the claim that faith has affectional dimensions and to clarify what those are.

---

11 The word "merely" is intended to affirm the biblical teaching that there is a "joy" (a kind of satisfaction) that *does* indeed *result*, or grow, from faith, such as the fruit of the Spirit in Gal. 5:22; but the word "merely" also is intended to affirm that other biblical teaching points to a kind of "joy" or "delight" or "satisfaction" or "treasuring" which we will find, in the coming pages, is an actual dimension of saving faith itself.

2

The "Free Will" Air We Breathe

I GREW UP IN A RELIGIOUS milieu whose assumptions distorted the nature of faith. That is, I grew up in the modern Western world. This milieu was marked by the de-supernaturalizing of Christianity. Conceptions of faith in the last two hundred years in the West have been shaped by views of human self-determination that dominate much of modern thinking—both secular and religious. This brings me to the second root of my concern with the question of the affectional aspect of saving faith.

Demand for Ultimate Self-Determination

The air we breathe is permeated by the assumption that human beings cannot be held responsible for their thoughts or feelings or actions, if they do not have ultimate self-determination. This assumption usually flourishes under the revered flag of "free will."

The term *free will* is a sacred and unassailable building block in our culture, including much of evangelicalism. It is seldom defined. But the all-controlling conviction is that the only meaningful freedom of the human soul is a freedom that has the power of ultimate self-determination. In other words, to be truly human and free, my will, not God's, must be decisive in whether I trust him.

My perception is that this pervasive assumption in our culture is a significant obstacle for people in grasping the true nature of saving faith and how it comes about. The assumption says that when I am told to have saving faith, I must have the power in myself to perform it. I cannot be decisively dependent on God at the instant of my conversion. Otherwise, I am not responsible to have the faith required. If God calls me to believe, then believing must be in my power decisively, not his, at the instant I exercise saving faith. This is what the assumption of ultimate self-determination requires.

Affectional Faith Is a Threat to Self-Determination

Therefore, for most people, the suggestion that saving faith might include an affectional change in the heart is perceived intuitively as wrong. It just can't *be*. We have no immediate control over the affections of our hearts. I control my *will*, they say, but not my *affections*. Therefore, God cannot command me to experience any particular affection—like being satisfied in Jesus, or delighting in Jesus, or treasuring Jesus above money and fame. Such affections cannot be required of me because I have no way in myself to make them happen.

I am not saying that most people think this through and articulate it. I am saying that the assumption of ultimate self-determination (flying under the flag of "free will") is so widespread and so deep that subconsciously most people incline toward views that leave the assumption intact.

My suggestion that saving faith involves an affectional dimension—like treasuring or cherishing or being satisfied—is instinctively ruled out, because humans don't have the power to change their affections and thus experience the required saving faith. It's too demanding. It calls for what I can't produce.

Redefining Faith as Manageable Decision

But clearly faith is required. It is commanded. "*Believe* in the Lord Jesus" (Acts 16:31). Therefore, the pervasive assumption of ultimate self-determination has led thousands of pastors and evangelists over the past few centuries to develop a kind of evangelism that fits with self-determining free will. A saving response to the gospel simply must be within the decisive control of the hearer, or else how can he be summoned to "obey the gospel," that is, to believe (2 Thess. 1:8; 1 Pet. 4:17)?

This has led to a primary focus on "decisions" in doing evangelism. What we call for in leading people to Christ is a "decision" for or against Christ. So saving faith—which is what people must have in order to be saved—comes to be viewed increasingly as a doable decision. Decisions are in our control—so we think. At least they are much more obviously doable than something like treasuring Christ or being satisfied in Christ. These spiritual affections are not only outside our immediate control, but also are less visible and demonstrable. Calling for such changes makes the work of the evangelist more dependent on miraculous changes in people's hearts and makes success less immediately discernible.

I grew up in the kind of Christianity where the assumption of self-determination had long ago produced this understanding of saving faith as a doable decision. I do not want to perpetuate the kind of religion that it so often produced. Many people around me were far better than their tacit theological assumptions, thank God. But the pull toward a de-supernaturalized faith was a pull not only toward what was doable, but also toward what was deadening.

Faith Is Not Manageable—It's a Miracle

I believe saving faith is a miracle. It is a gift of God (Eph. 2:8; Phil 1:29). People—all of us at one point—who are dead in sin cannot perform this miracle. We must be raised from the dead by God (Eph. 2:5). The fact that we are spiritually dead and blind in our rebellion against God does not remove our accountability. We are responsible to believe, and we must be born again in order to believe. "Everyone who believes that Jesus is the Christ *has been* born of God" (1 John 5:1). Faith is the living sign that we have been born again. The miracle of the new birth brings faith into existence. Therefore, the Bible does not allow the argument that, in order to be accountable before God, faith must be a doable decision. Before it is doable by me, it must be given by God. My ultimate self-determination is not a biblical assumption.

We all are influenced by where we come from. This is surely true for me. Having grown up in a milieu that diminished the supernatural nature of conversion, and elevated man as decisive in the act of saving faith, and turned faith into a doable decision, I have felt a decades-long drive to dig into the nature of saving faith. What are the affectional elements of faith? Is saving faith an affectional embrace of Christ? Is it the receiving of Christ as a treasure? Indeed, is it the treasuring of Christ?

3

Why I Am Not a Roman Catholic

MY THIRD AND FOURTH REASONS for being drawn to the affectional aspect of saving faith are, in a sense, one reason. I want to understand how saving faith can have an affectional dimension, like treasuring Christ, without undermining the historic Protestant doctrine of justification by faith alone. How can I own up to the affectional aspect of saving faith that I see in the Bible without smuggling into faith a kind of meritorious virtue that would turn justification by faith alone into justification by human goodness or holiness?

Wrestling with that one question, however, has resulted in the need to battle on two fronts. On the one hand, I don't agree with the way Roman Catholics deal with the question. On the other hand, I don't agree with the way Sandemanianism deals with it either. Roman Catholics have no problem treating saving faith as affectional because they treat saving faith, understood as a virtue, as part of justification-sanctification, which I hyphenate because Roman Catholics consider sanctification as part of justification.[1] Robert Sandeman (1718–1771)

---

1 For another angle on the Roman Catholic understanding of the connection between justification (which I define as God's once-for-all act of declaring us righteous on our first

solved the problem by removing all affectional dimensions from saving faith and treating it as "bare assent to the work of Christ."[2]

As I read the Bible, neither of these views is right. So my understanding of saving faith has brought me into conflict with both. That is why there is a third and fourth reason for my engagement with the question of the affectional nature of saving faith—one dealt with in this chapter, one in the next.

Saving Faith Is Good

The third reason relates to the Roman Catholic understanding of justification by faith. I need to deal with this because some will think my treatment of saving faith is a kind of courtship with Rome, which it emphatically is not. So how then do I treat saving faith as having an affectional dimension without getting on the road to Rome?

I don't solve this problem by denying that saving faith is a good thing. It pleases God that we believe (Heb. 11:6). In fact, I think this can be said of every biblical description of faith. Saving faith is never a vice. It is never evil. If someone has saving faith, it is good that he does. But this does not mean that we are justified by our goodness. I will argue that in justifying us, God does not do it with a view to any goodness in our faith.

Legitimate Concern of Roman Catholicism

When the Reformers like Martin Luther and John Calvin preached justification by faith alone, the Roman Catholics feared that this

---

authentic act of saving faith) and sanctification (which I define as the ongoing work of the Holy Spirit in making us holy in our hearts and minds and actions), see John Piper, "No Love Lost: How Catholics (and Some Protestants) Go Wrong on Good Works," February 26, 2018, Desiring God website, https://www.desiringgod.org/.

2 See Wayne Grudem, *"Free Grace" Theology: 5 Ways It Diminishes the Gospel* (Wheaton, IL: Crossway, 2016), 34n10.

doctrine would lead to lives without obedience or holiness or love. You can hear their concern in the Roman Catholic documents of the Council of Trent (1545–1563):

> No one, how much soever justified, ought to think himself exempt from the observance of the commandments. (chapter 11)

> If anyone saith, that nothing besides faith is commanded in the Gospel; that other things are indifferent, neither commanded nor prohibited, but free; or, that the ten commandments nowise appertain to Christians; let him be anathema. (canon 14)

> If anyone saith, that the man who is justified and how perfect soever, is not bound to observe the commandments of God and of the Church . . . let him be anathema. (canon 20)[3]

These statements are legitimate warnings against an unbiblical view of justification by faith alone. It is true that obedience must and will mark the person who is genuinely justified by saving faith. Or to say it another way: sanctification always follows justification. No exceptions. Faith without works is dead. Such faith does not justify (Gal. 5:6; James 2:14, 26).

Conflation of Justification and Sanctification Is Not the Answer

The way the Roman Catholic Church has attempted to secure the link between justification and sanctification is by conflating them,

---

3 *The Council of Trent: The Sixth Session*, trans. J. Waerworth (London: Dolman, 1848), 30–53, accessed June 21, 2021, https://history.hanover.edu/.

which the Reformers considered a loss of the gospel. For example, the Council of Trent puts it like this in the Decree on Justification:

> Justification . . . is not remission of sins merely, but also the sanctification and renewal of the inward man. (chapter 7)

This is what I mean by the conflation of justification and sanctification. It follows, then, for Roman Catholicism, that our justification, like our sanctification, is progressive. It may grow. We may be "further justified" since justification consists in our own measure of goodness brought about graciously in the new birth:

> They, through the observance of the commandments of God and of the Church, faith co-operating with good works, *increase in that righteousness* which they have received through the grace of Christ, and are still *further justified*. (chapter 10; emphasis added)[4]

It follows, then, that Roman Catholicism sees saving faith as part of sanctification itself. The Council of Trent says, "Faith, unless hope and charity be added thereto, neither unites man perfectly with Christ, nor makes him a living member of His body" (chapter 7). What they mean by that statement is that "hope and charity" don't merely follow faith as fruit, but are added to it as constituents. Faith is "formed" by love, as they say. Love (including love for neighbor) is part of it. That is the way they construe Galatians 5:6: "In Christ Jesus neither circumcision nor uncircumcision counts for anything, but only *faith working through love*."

---

4 The puzzling phrase "further justified" fits into the Roman Catholic view that to be justified is to be "made righteous" (*impartation* by the Holy Spirit), while the Reformed view is that to be justified is to be "declared righteous" (*imputation* of Christ's perfect righteousness).

Roman Catholic theology traditionally construes the love in Galatians 5:6 as love to both God and neighbor, and then argues that such love gives faith its justifying effectiveness. This faith-forming love is emphatically not what I am referring to when I speak in this book about treasuring Christ as part of saving faith. I do not see love for neighbor as part of justifying faith. It is the fruit of faith, not what faith is.

I will explore in what sense we may speak of love to Christ as treasuring Christ. But when I speak of loving Christ as treasuring Christ and, in that sense, part of justifying faith, I am not basing this on Galatians 5:6. In fact, I think the main focus in Galatians 5:6 is on neighbor love, not love for God or Christ. When Paul refers to *faith working through love*, I think he means that faith is the kind of reality that gives rise to love for other people.[5]

For Roman Catholicism, therefore, one does not speak of how faith leads to justification and sanctification. Rather one says that faith is part of justification (and sanctification), as are all other graces infused into the soul by God. In Catholicism, one is not justified by faith, as though justification and faith were distinct things. Rather, the free grace of justification (Trent, chapter 8) is mediated sacramentally through baptism, and consists in the virtue of faith formed by love. In this way, Catholicism hopes to preserve the connection between justification, faith, and holiness of life. They are inseparable because they are merged into one.

Protestants Are Right to Protest

I do not think this way of understanding saving faith, and this way of holding justification and sanctification together, is what

---

5 See chap. 11 for a discussion of how faith is the root of all God-pleasing works and for a fuller discussion of Gal. 5:6 and why I think the *love* in this verse refers to love for neighbor, not love for God or Christ.

the Bible teaches. I think the Protestant Reformers were right to protest. My aim here is to clarify that when I find in the Bible an affectional dimension in saving faith, you will understand that I do not think this undermines the traditional Reformed understanding of justification by faith alone.[6]

The Bible teaches that justification is an act of God experienced by those whom God views as "ungodly." In other words, justification is not the *infusion* of godliness but the *counting* of an ungodly person as righteous:

> Now to the one who works, his wages are not counted as a gift but as his due. And to the one who does not work but believes in him who *justifies the ungodly*, his faith is counted as righteousness. (Rom. 4:4–5)

This does not mean that "believing" is an ungodly act. It means that when a person is "born of God," and brought from spiritual death to living faith (1 John 5:1), in that instant God's justifying act does not have respect to *believing as a virtue*, but to believing *as a receiving of Christ*, in whom the believer is counted righteous (see Rom. 3:24–25).

Paul is at pains in Philippians 3:8–9 to distinguish his own righteousness from the righteousness that we have in union with Christ by faith alone:

> For his sake I have suffered the loss of all things and count them as rubbish, in order that I may gain Christ and be found *in him,*

6 For a full exposition and defense of my understanding of justification, see John Piper, *Counted Righteous in Christ: Should We Abandon the Imputation of Christ's Righteousness?* (Wheaton, IL: Crossway, 2002); and *The Future of Justification: A Response to N. T. Wright* (Wheaton, IL: Crossway, 2007). See also Piper, "No Love Lost," from which several paragraphs in this section are taken.

not having a righteousness of my own that comes from the law, but that which comes through faith in Christ, *the righteousness from God that depends on faith.*

In this text, the righteousness we have "in him" and the righteousness we have "through faith in Christ" are the same. Therefore, we understand that faith is the instrument by which God unites us to Christ, where we enjoy a righteousness, by imputation, that is not our own.

Justification Based on Christ Alone through Faith Alone

I infer, therefore, that when Paul says that God "justifies the ungodly" (Rom. 4:5), he implies that justification is not sanctification. It is not a process of emerging godliness. Justification is not God's imparting to me, or infusing in me, a righteousness that I perform. It is an instantaneous act of acquittal and vindication. It is an instantaneous act of counting a person perfectly righteous who is not righteous in and of himself. The ground of this declaration is not in us, but in Christ. That is justification by faith—saving faith.

So I do not follow the Roman Catholic way of relating faith to justification. But neither do I follow the way of the Sandemanians, who say that saving faith is a "bare assent to the work of Christ." Rome errs by merging faith as a virtue with justification, which then merges with sanctification. Sandemanianism errs by stripping faith of any affectional (and thus virtuous) dimension. Dealing with Robert Sandeman proved to be very fruitful in my concern with the nature of saving faith in relation to justification. So that is where we turn next.

4

If Saving Faith Is Affectional,
Does It Merit Justification?

IF THE RELATIONSHIP BETWEEN saving faith and justification is not what Roman Catholicism says it is, and yet saving faith, with its affectional elements, really is a good thing, not a sin, how does it not creep into the *ground* of justification as something virtuous? Or how does the "goodness" of saving faith not contaminate the *instrument* of justification with meritorious virtue?

This chapter deals with my fourth reason for digging into the affectional nature of saving faith—namely, my desire to see how justification by faith alone comes about when faith itself includes virtuous affectional elements. The crucial insight became clear as I dealt with Sandemanianism. Or to be more accurate, it became clear as I followed the way Andrew Fuller dealt with Sandemanianism.

Clarifying Sandemanianism

I don't expect most readers to know what Sandemanianism is or who Andrew Fuller is. The reason I bring up this 250-year-old

47

view (that most people today have never even heard of) is because in answering it, we also discover why the affectional nature of saving faith does not undermine justification by faith alone. In other words, the answer to Sandemanianism is also the answer to Roman Catholicism. The answer that Andrew Fuller (1754–1815) gave to Robert Sandeman (1718–1771) provides the key to why saving faith is more than "a bare assent to the work of Christ" and yet does not undermine justification by faith alone, or turn me into a Roman Catholic.

Let me see if I can explain. I hope you will take a few minutes to go back with me a couple of centuries for the sake of an extremely important insight. Sandemanianism was named after Robert Sandeman, a Scottish pastor, who held that "bare assent to the work of Christ is alone necessary" for justification.[1] In other words, while Roman Catholicism tries to make sure saving faith is never without good works, Sandemanians try to protect saving faith from any intermingling of good works. I share both of these concerns. It is biblical to do so.

Catholics tried to preserve godliness by making it part of justification. Sandemanians tried to preserve the justification of the ungodly (Rom. 4:5) by excluding any affectional dimension from saving faith. Catholics feared that if godliness were not part of justification, Christians would be lawless. Sandemanians feared that if godliness were part of saving faith, the truth of justification would vanish.

Fuller's Insightful Response

I have never found a more trenchant corrective to Sandemanianism than the British Baptist pastor and theologian Andrew Fuller,

---

1   Wayne Grudem, *"Free Grace" Theology: 5 Ways It Diminishes the Gospel* (Wheaton, IL: Crossway, 2016), 34.

the "rope holder" for the famous missionary William Carey. Here's how he describes Sandemanianism. Its distinguishing marks relate

> to the nature of justifying faith. Sandeman constantly repre-
> sents [justifying faith] as the bare belief of the bare truth; by
> which definition he intends, as it would seem, to exclude from
> it everything *pertaining to the will and the affections*, except as
> effects produced by it. . . . "Everyone," says he, "who obtains a
> just notion of the person and work of Christ, or whose notion
> corresponds to what is testified of him, is justified, and finds
> peace with God simply by that notion."
>
> This notion he considers as the effect of truth being impressed
> upon the mind, and denies that the mind is active in it. "He who
> maintains," says he, "that we are justified only by faith, and at the
> same time affirms . . . that faith is a work exerted by the human
> mind, undoubtedly maintains, if he had any meaning to his words,
> that we are justified by a work exerted by the human mind."[2]

Notice the word *affections*. Sandeman's aim is to "exclude from [saving faith] everything pertaining to the will *and the affections*." Why? Because he believes that if the will or the affections is involved in saving faith, then faith will be a human act of goodness or godliness, which would seem to mean that justification by faith is justification by human goodness—by works.

You can see why this view draws my attention. What I find in the Bible is, in fact, an affectional aspect of saving faith. So if

---

2 Andrew Fuller, *Strictures on Sandemanianism*, in *The Complete Works of Andrew Fuller*, (Harrisonburg, VA: Sprinkle, 1988), 2:266–67; emphasis added. Several paragraphs in this section about Fuller are adapted from John Piper, *Andrew Fuller: Holy Faith, Worthy Gospel, World Missions* (Wheaton, IL: Crossway, 2016).

Sandeman is right, then my view would undermine justification by faith alone. So I am eager to answer both Roman Catholicism and Sandemanianism. From two different sides, both of them are ready to say "Gotcha!" when they hear me say that saving faith includes an affectional dimension like treasuring Christ. Catholics would say "Gotcha" because they think I'm in their camp. Sandemanians would say "Gotcha" because they think I've left Christianity.[3]

Pillar Text for Robert Sandeman

Sandeman's main support for his view is the meaning of the term *ungodly* in Romans 4:5: "To the one who does not work but believes in him who justifies the *ungodly*, his faith is counted as righteousness." Sandeman argues that the word *ungodly* must mean that there is no godly or virtuous quality about saving faith, for if there were, we would not be called ungodly as we are being justified by faith. This is why he defines faith as a passive persuasion of the truth in which the mind is not active in any virtuous way. So faith can coexist with ungodliness, understood as the total absence of any godly act of the soul.[4] Thus Romans 4:5, he would say, stands as true and supports his view.

Fuller's Decisive Insight

How Andrew Fuller responds to this argument provides one of the most important insights of the book you are reading. I am happy to give him credit. Of course, others have seen it. But

---

3 Sandeman took his view so seriously that he saw the mainstream Puritan writers (including men like Flavel, Boston, Guthrie, and the Erskines) as furnishing "a devout path to hell." Fuller, *Strictures on Sandemanianism*, 566.
4 Fuller, *Strictures on Sandemanianism*, 568.

Fuller has helped me see it more clearly than any other. His basic point is that saving faith is, in fact, a virtuous act of the soul, not a sin, but that *in justifying us God considers faith not as human goodness or holiness but as a reception of Christ, whose righteousness alone is the ground of our justification.* I agree with this. And I will let him speak for himself:

> This term [*ungodly* in Rom. 4:5] . . . is not designed, in the passage under consideration, to express the actual state of mind which the party at the time possesses, but the character under which God considers him in bestowing the blessing of justification upon him. Whatever be the present state of the sinner's mind—whether he be a haughty Pharisee or a humble publican—if he possess nothing which can in any degree balance the curse which stands against him, or at all operate as a ground of acceptance with God, he must be justified, if at all, as unworthy, ungodly, and wholly out of regard to the righteousness of the mediator.[5]

He uses the analogy of a compass to help us see that faith can have certain qualities (like the affectional dimension of treasuring Christ) that God nevertheless does not consider, or take into account, when he reckons faith as justifying:

> Whatever holiness there is in [faith], it is not this, but the obedience of Christ, that constitutes our justifying righteousness. Whatever other properties the magnet [compass] may possess, it is as pointing invariably to the north that it guides the mariner;

---

5 Andrew Fuller, *Expositions Miscellaneous*, in *The Complete Works of Andrew Fuller*, 3:715.

and whatever other properties faith may possess, it is as receiving Christ, and bringing us into union with him, that it justifies.[6]

"Peculiarly Receiving Grace"

This insight is foundational for my thinking in this book. When considering saving faith as the human instrument of justification, God does not focus on the holiness, or goodness, or beauty, or virtue of faith, as though such qualities could merit or woo the grace of reckoning a sinner perfectly righteous. Rather, God focuses on faith as "peculiarly a receiving grace." That is Andrew Fuller's term. Here's how he explains it:

> Justification is ascribed to faith, because it is by faith that we receive Christ; and thus it is by faith only, and not by any other grace. Faith is *peculiarly a receiving grace* which none other is. Were we said to be justified by repentance, by love,[7] or by any other grace, it would convey to us the idea of something good in us being the consideration on which the blessing was bestowed; but justification by faith conveys no such idea. On the contrary, it leads the mind directly to Christ, in the same manner as saying of a person that he lives by begging leads to the idea of his living on what he freely receives.[8]

So it turns out that Sandeman was wrong. The fact that faith may have an affectional dimension does not prove that justifica-

---

6 Andrew Fuller, *Memoirs, Sermons, Etc.*, in *The Complete Works of Andrew Fuller*, 1:281.

7 As I understand him, Fuller does not mean that every sort of love is excluded from justifying faith, but rather what is excluded is any love conceived of as a "giving grace" rather than a "receiving grace." Love considered as the humble *reception* of Christ as lovely in his saving work is not excluded. Thus, I don't see myself as in disagreement with Fuller at this point.

8 Fuller, *Memoirs, Sermons, Etc.*, 282; emphasis added.

tion then would be by works, or on the basis of our virtue. The justification of the ungodly in Roman 4:5 does *not* exclude from the experience of the ungodly the "peculiarly receiving grace" of faith.[9]

On the contrary, when we think about the justification of the ungodly in Romans 4:5, what matters is not that there be no spiritual affections in our faith (like treasuring Christ or being satisfied in Christ), "but that, whatever we possess we make nothing of it as a ground of acceptance, 'counting all things but loss and dung that we may . . . be found in him.'"[10]

Faith is good. Hebrews 11:6 says, "Without faith it is impossible to please [God]." Surely, then, faith is pleasing to God. "Yet," as Fuller says, "it is not as such, but as uniting us to Christ and deriving righteousness from him, that it justifies."[11] Faith does not cease to be "peculiarly a receiving grace" just because it is the receiving of Christ *as a supreme treasure.*

---

9 Not to burden the reader with excessive argumentation in the text, I add two more solid exegetical observations from Andrew Fuller about Rom. 4:5. Observation 1: "Neither Abraham nor David, whose cases the apostle selects for the illustration of his argument, was, at the time referred to, the enemy of God. . . . But the truth is, [Abraham] had been a believer in God and a true worshiper of him for many years, at the time when he is said to have believed in God, and it was counted to him for righteousness, Genesis 12:1–3 15:6; Hebrews 11:8. Here then is an account of one who had walked with God for a series of years 'working not, but believing on him that justifieth the ungodly;' a clear proof that by 'working not' the apostle did not mean a wicked inaction, but a renunciation of works as the ground of acceptance with God" (Fuller, *Expositions Miscellaneous*, 717). Observation 2: "It has been said that the term *ungodly* is never used but to describe the party as being under *actual enmity* of God at the time. I apprehend this is a mistake. Christ is said to have died for the 'ungodly.' Did he then lay down his life only for those who, *at the time*, were actually his enemies? If so, he did not die for any of the Old Testament saints, nor for any of the godly who were then alive, nor even for his own apostles. All that can in truth be said is that whatever were the characters at the time, he died for them *as* ungodly; and thus it is that he 'justifieth the ungodly'" (Fuller, *Strictures on Sandemanianism*, 404).

10 Fuller, *Strictures on Sandemanianism*, 406.

11 Fuller, *Strictures on Sandemanianism*, 572.

Bright Guide between Catholicism and Sandeman

Fuller's insight is foundational to my argument in this book. It is the light that guides us along the narrow way between the errors of Roman Catholicism and Sandemanianism. It protects from Catholicism by showing that justification is not a work of God *in* us, but a work of God *for* us as we are united to Christ through faith alone. Faith is not an infused part of sanctification called justification. Faith is the reception of Christ, whose righteousness is counted as ours, without which we would perish as ungodly.

And this insight protects us from Sandemanianism—a bare intellectual "faith"—by showing us that faith can have affectional aspects that do not undermine justification by faith alone. Such faith does not undermine justification by faith alone, because God does not have respect to any virtuousness of the affectional aspects of faith, but only to faith as "uniting us to Christ," who is the sole ground of our right standing with God.

Fuller's insights are so crucial and so far-reaching, I want to let him say it one more time. He celebrates the message of the New Testament preachers like this:

> The ground on which they took their stand was "Cursed is everyone who continueth not in all things written in the book of the law to do them" [Gal. 3:10]. Hence they inferred the impossibility of the sinner being justified in any other way than for the sake of him who was "made a curse for us;" and hence it clearly follows, that whatever holiness any sinner may possess before, in, or after believing, it is of no account whatever as a ground of acceptance with God.[12]

12 Fuller, *Strictures on Sandemanianism*, 393.

54

So my fourth reason (like the third) for being drawn to the issue of whether faith is an affectional embrace (a receiving!) of Christ has been the desire to discover the affectional nature of saving faith without undermining the biblical doctrine of justification by faith alone. I wanted to discover the biblical way of owning up to the affectional aspect of saving faith without turning faith into an infused constituent of justification, and without denying the justification of the *ungodly.*

As Andrew Fuller, from two hundred years ago, became my guide into a clearer, deeper understanding of justification by faith, so others from church history have done the same. In fact, the provocative statements that prominent Protestant theologians have made about saving faith over the centuries may be described as my fifth reason for pressing into the affectional nature of saving faith. In chapter 5, I will give you a taste of these mentors.

5

Provocative Voices from Church History

THE FIFTH REASON I am drawn to probe the Scriptures about the affectional nature of saving faith is that great voices in the history of Protestant thought have pointed in this direction. These are the long-dead mentors I mentioned in the introduction who provoke me and help me.

It goes almost without saying that Roman Catholic thinkers speak about the affections as constitutive of faith—in a very different sense than I do. That tradition has not drawn me to the issue. I have shown already that the Roman Catholic treatment of faith undermines the biblical teaching on justification.[1] Therefore, this tradition has held little attraction for me. But the Protestant theologians who deal with the affectional dimensions of saving faith stir me up to go to the Scriptures to see if these things are so (Acts 17:11).

1 See chap. 3.

Three Elements of Saving Faith

The most common way to describe the nature of saving faith in the Protestant tradition is to focus on three elements, often named with their Latin roots: knowledge (*notitia*), assent (*assensus*), and trust (*fiducia*).[2] Looking back on centuries of Protestant thought, Herman Bavinck (1854–1921) describes the three elements and how they relate to salvation:

> Though faith was considered as a kind of knowledge (*notitia* . . .) and intellectual assent (*assensus* . . .), it was above all a willing trust (*fiducia* . . .). This was not a general belief that God exists and that forgiveness and salvation are present in Christ, but a special confidence that forgiveness and salvation have also been granted to me personally.[3]

The very fact that the plural *elements* or *aspects* has been used for centuries to describe faith is a pointer that my question in this book is not quirky. I am asking about an affectional *dimension* or *element* or *aspect* of saving faith. This is what the church has long attempted to do in defining the nature of faith—she has inquired

2 In the words of Benjamin Warfield, "Protestant theologians have generally explained that faith includes in itself the three elements of *notitia, assensus, fiducia*. . . . No doubt theologians have differed among themselves as to whether all these elements are to be counted as included in faith, or some of them treated rather as preliminary steps to faith or effects of faith. But speaking broadly Protestant theologians have reckoned all these elements as embraced within the mental movement we call faith itself; and they have obviously been right in so doing." *Works of Benjamin B. Warfield: Studies in Theology*, vol. 9 (Bellingham, WA: Logos Bible Software, 2008), 340–41. Herman Bavinck traces these three back to Melanchthon in the Protestant tradition. Herman Bavinck, John Bolt, and John Vriend, *Reformed Dogmatics: Holy Spirit, Church, and New Creation*, vol. 4 (Grand Rapids, MI: Baker Academic, 2008), 113.

3 Bavinck, Bolt, and Vriend, *Reformed Dogmatics*, 110–11.

into what the Bible reveals as *elements* that go into making saving faith what it is.[4]

Three Elements Have Never Been Enough

But it would be a mistake to think that Protestant theologians have been satisfied with the explanatory power of only three elements of saving faith. The scope of *believing*, as found in Scripture, is too broad and diverse to be exhausted by *knowledge*, *assent*, and *trust*. Moreover, each of these three elements may be queried more closely and deeply as to what each of them actually signifies in real experience.

Hence, we will see that notable Christian theologians have found more than three elements of saving faith. For example, Francis Turretin (1623–1687) found six acts of the soul in saving faith, and Hermann Witsius (1636–1708) found eight. And the more I read those who have thought most carefully about the nature of saving faith, the more common it becomes that they all point to elements of saving faith that are *affectional*.[5]

Before wading into these historical waters, let me remind you about the function of this chapter in the book. The first sentence in the chapter is this: "The fifth reason I am drawn to probe the Scriptures about the affectional nature of saving faith is that great

---

4 It would not be accurate to say that my proposal in this book is that we add a fourth element to the traditional three: knowing, assenting, trusting—and treasuring. More accurate would be to say that my proposal is that for *knowing* to be saving, it must be a knowing of Christ as a treasure, and for *assenting* to be saving, it must be assenting to Christ as a treasure, and for *trust* to be saving, it must be a treasuring trust.

5 Of course, this selection of voices from history is limited. There are many more. Just one more example: "Evangelical faith is an act of both the understanding and the will. It is complex, involving a spiritual perception of Christ and *an affectionate love of him*." William Greenough Thayer Shedd, *Dogmatic Theology*, ed. Alan W. Gomes, 3rd ed. (Phillipsburg, NJ: P&R, 2003), 788; emphasis added.

voices in the history of Protestant thought have pointed in this direction." In other words, I am *not* referring to these historical voices to support my point. I think they do. But that's not the point. The point is that the way they talk about faith provokes me to go to the Scriptures to see if faith has an affectional element. This means that even if I am wrong about some of these historical voices, it doesn't determine the validity of what I find in Scripture. The voices are not argument. They are incentives to look for arguments in the Bible.

Calvin: "Pious Affection"

Let's start with John Calvin (1509–1564). In his *Commentary on Ephesians*, he ponders the nature of faith in Paul's prayer that pleads that Christ "may dwell in your hearts through faith" (Eph. 3:17). He writes:

> By faith we not only acknowledge that Christ suffered and rose from the dead on our account, but, accepting the offers which he makes of himself, *we possess and enjoy him* as our Savior. . . . In a word, faith is not a distant view, but *a warm embrace of Christ*, by which he dwells in us, and we are filled with the Divine Spirit.[6]

One might quibble and say that, for Calvin, the reference to *possessing and enjoying Christ* is experienced "by faith" but is not part of faith itself. But it is difficult to exclude *enjoying Christ* from the nature of faith when he says, "Faith *is* . . . a warm embrace of Christ." He does not say that faith "results in" but "is" this "warm embrace."

---

6   John Calvin and William Pringle, *Commentaries of the Epistles of Paul to the Galatians and Ephesians* (Bellingham, WA: Logos Bible Software, 2010), 262; emphasis added.

In the *Institutes*, he presses into the meaning of *assent*. How is this actually experienced in reality? He answers:

> Assent itself . . . *is more a matter of the heart than the head, of the affection than the intellect*. . . . As there can be no doubt on the matter, we in one word conclude, that they talk absurdly when they maintain that faith is formed by the addition of pious affection as an accessory to assent, since *assent itself, such at least as the Scriptures describe, consists in pious affection*. . . . Therefore *faith cannot possibly be disjoined from pious affection*.[7]

"Enjoy." "Warm embrace." "Pious affection." These are the kinds of faith-defining phrases that send me to the Scriptures with eyes wide open to see what Calvin saw. Or not.

Turretin: "Embracing That Inestimable Treasure"

Francis Turretin (1623–1687) was born fifty-nine years after the death of John Calvin. He served as a pastor for almost forty years in Geneva and then as a professor of theology at the University of Geneva. In his *Institutes of Elenctic Theology*, Turretin finds at least six acts in the experience of saving faith.[8]

He acknowledges the common view that faith consists in knowledge, assent, and trust, but he says that we will understand faith more fully if "we treat more distinctly of them." By "more distinctly," he means by breaking them down into six elements, not

---

7 John Calvin, *Institutes of the Christian Religion*, trans. Henry Beveridge, 2 vols. (Edinburgh: Calvin Translation Society, 1845), 3.2.8.

8 Francis Turretin, *Institutes of Elenctic Theology*, ed. James T. Dennison Jr., trans. George Musgrave Giger, vol. 2 (Phillipsburg, NJ: P&R, 1992–1997), 561–64. All page numbers after Turretin's quotes are from this source. This odd word, *elenctic*, has to do with teaching, or persuading, or convicting, or bringing someone to a new position.

just three. "These acts of faith are not of one kind, but various and multiple, according to its various relations" (561).[9]

The first is the act of *knowledge* (*notitia*). "As truth is the object of faith . . . , it requires, above all, knowledge for its apprehension" (561). Second, we experience "*theoretical assent* by which we receive as true and divine what we know" (561). Third, we experience "*fiducial and practical assent*, by which we judge the gospel to be not only true, but also good and therefore most worthy of our love and desire" (562). Fourth, faith "is an *act of refuge* . . . by which we betake ourselves by an act of desire to Christ . . . seeking in him pardon of sin and salvation" (562).

The fifth act of faith is supremely important. Turretin calls it "the formal and principal act of justifying faith." His description of it is so full of *affectional* reality that I quote it more fully:

> The fifth is the act of *reception of Christ* . . . by which we not only seek Christ through a desire of the soul . . . but *embrace*

9   The term *acts of faith* is ambiguous. In common parlance, it may refer to a brave act, like risking your life to speak the gospel to an enemy of Christ. That is *not* what is meant by the phrase in this chapter, as we discuss the nature of faith in the minds of these historical figures. *Acts of faith*, as I am using the term in this chapter, are not actions that *result from* faith. They are what faith itself, in itself, as itself, does. I confess that while some distinguish the various aspects of faith's *nature* from the various aspects of faith's *acting*, I do not. I simply cannot see any distinction. The ambiguity arises from the fact it is odd to speak of the *acts of faith* because we hear that phrase in the same way we hear the phrase *acts of the soul*. The soul, with its perceiving and volitional capacities, is not identical with its acts. It has being prior to its believing. But faith is not like that. Faith is one of the acts of the soul. Therefore, it *is* act. It does not *do* acts. This is why the phrase *acts of faith* is confusing. So when I use the term *acts of faith*, I am referring to the various actings that constitute what faith *is*. Its nature is its various actings. Theologians have asked whether faith exists when it is not in action. For example, are we believing—do we have faith—when we are asleep? Or when we are wholly engaged in solving a difficult math problem? Some have suggested at this point the concept of the *habitus* of faith. But as best I can understand such a concept, it winds up identifying faith's *habitus* with the new nature we are given in regeneration, which secures the abiding reality of faith when we are conscious.

him. For as God freely offers his own Son in the gospel to the sinful soul . . . so the soul . . . cannot help embracing . . . *that supreme good offered, and the inestimable treasure,* selling all for him (Mt. 13:44), resting upon Christ . . . *prepared to lose anything else rather than reject him.* This is the formal and principal act of justifying faith, usually termed *"reception"*: "As many as received him" (i.e., "who believed on his name," Jn. 1:12). (563; emphasis added)

If Turretin is right, you can see why I am so eager to write this book. What does it mean to be a Christian? It means believing on Christ, not by a bare decision to affirm that Christ can rescue us from hell and make our future more like a golf course than a forest fire. That is not saving faith. To become a Christian—to be justified and finally saved—is to "embrace Christ." Embrace! Not take between the fingers as one gets a boarding pass, shows it twice, and then, after the flight, throws it away. Faith does not "embrace" Christ briefly with mere fingers. To believe savingly is to embrace Christ with the soul as the "supreme good offered, and the inestimable treasure." Believing is receiving—receiving Christ not as a guardian of my most treasured possessions, but as the most precious possession himself, for which I am "prepared to lose anything." This is what it means to be a Christian. Yes. I do think Turretin is right.

Turrretin's sixth act of faith is simply the act of looking at what has transpired in our own heart and marveling (believing) that we have been brought to faith. He calls it *"the reflex act* arising from a sense of faith by which the soul which has thus received Christ . . . concludes that it believes and, because it believes, that Christ certainly died for him and belongs to him with all his blessings and that he will assuredly be made happy by him" (563). Such a (reflex) sight of our own faith, and its confirmation in our life, is not unlike what we see in Paul's argument in Romans 5:3–5 and in Peter's argument in 2 Peter 1:9–11. The life of faith feeds on Christ but is also confirmed and strengthened by its own existence and fruit.

Witsius: "A Hunger and Thirst after Christ"

Hermann Witsius (1636–1708) was a Dutch pastor and theologian who taught at the universities of Franeker, Utrecht, and Leiden. He states a reason for why he and others found it necessary to speak of faith as various acts of the soul, rather than as a simple thing:

[Saving faith] is not any one particular act or habit, nor must it be restricted to any one particular faculty of the soul, for it is a certain complex thing, consisting of various acts, which, without confusion pervade, and by a sweet and happy conjunction, mutually promote and assist one another; it imports a change of the whole man, is the spring of the whole spiritual life, and in fine, the holy energy and activity of the whole soul towards God, in Christ. And therefore its full extent can scarcely be distinctly comprehended under any one single idea.[10]

I think this is right. But I would want to quickly clarify that this does not imply, as one might suppose, that in our evangelism we must lay out *all* the dimensions of faith in order for a person to believe on Christ in a saving way. In evangelism, we often say, "Be-

---

10 Herman Witsius, *The Economy of the Covenants between God and Man: Comprehending a Complete Body of Divinity*, trans. William Crookshank, vol. 1 (London: T. Tegg & Son, 1837), 337. All page numbers after Witsius's quotes are from this source.

lieve in the Lord Jesus, and you will be saved" (Acts 16:31). And we describe who Jesus is and what he has done, not in an exhaustive way, but as seems wisest at the moment. We trust the Holy Spirit to bring a person's heart to receive Christ in a way that suits the reality of the truth that the mind and heart see.

But for the pastor and the growing Christian, who spend decades discovering the breadth and length and height and depth of what it is to know and trust and love Christ—for us, it will not do to pretend that hundreds of passages of Scripture can be adequately applied to our lives without pondering the diversity and relationships of faith's various dimensions. In fact, I would say that the more deeply we comprehend the multiple facets of the diamond of saving faith, the more readily and joyfully and effectively we will be able to share the good news in simple and comprehensible ways with unbelievers.

In this spirit, I cite Witsius's eight facets of saving faith.

1. "The first thing which faith either comprehends or presupposes, is the *knowledge* of the thing to be believed" (340).
2. "To this knowledge must be joined *assent*, which is the *second* act of faith, whereby a person receives and acknowledges as truths those things which he knows" (341).
3. "That which follows this assent is *the love of the truth thus known and acknowledged*; and this is the third act of faith, of which the apostle speaks, 2 Thess. 2:10" (344; emphasis added).

So at this point, Witsius introduces *love* for what is proclaimed in the gospel, as in 2 Thessalonians 2:10: "[They] are perishing, because they did not receive *a love of the truth* and so be saved" (my translation). He says that this love "is the third act of faith." Then he pauses to qualify. He says:

> It is indeed true that love, strictly speaking, is distinguished from faith; yet the acts of both graces are *so interwoven with one another, that we can neither explain nor exercise faith without some acts of love interfering.* . . . If any will call this love . . . a commanded act of faith, he is indeed welcome to do so . . . if he only maintain that it is not possible but the believing soul, while in the exercise of faith, must sincerely love the truth as it is in Christ . . . delighting itself in that truth: far otherwise than the devils and wicked men, who, what they know to be true, they could wish to be false. (345)

In other words, Witsius sees in 2 Thessalonians 2:10 a pointer to the difference between devils, who know that the gospel is true (but hate it), and believers, who know the gospel is true and receive it with love and with joy. A literal translation of 2 Thessalonians 2:10 is that unbelievers are perishing "because they did not *receive* the love of the truth that they may be saved." We will discuss later whether this "receiving" of love for gospel truth should be seen as an essential part of faith or not.[11] But suffice it to say now that Witsius has stirred me up to pursue this crucial question.

4. Witsius identifies the fourth act of faith as "a hunger and thirst after Christ" (345).
5. "This hunger and thirst are followed by *a receiving of Christ* the Lord for justification, sanctification, and so for complete

---

11 See chap. 18 for the positive exegesis where I deal with 2 Thess. 2:9–12 and faith as a kind of love for the truth.

salvation, which is the fifth, and indeed, the formal and principal act of faith" (345).

6. Then, revealing how there are no clear and distinct lines between these acts of faith, Witsius says, "If you would subtly distinguish this act of the believing soul, . . . reclining and thus staying itself upon Christ, from the act of receiving Christ, and make it posterior thereto, I shall not oppose it. Let us therefore call this the sixth act of faith" (346).

7. "When the believer so receives Christ and leans upon him, he not only considers him as a Savior, but also as a Lord. For he receives a whole Christ, and receiveth him just as he is: but he is no less Lord than a Savior. Yea, he cannot be a Savior, unless he be likewise a Lord. . . . And this our *surrender to Christ*, which we account the seventh act of faith, is the continual fountain and spring of all true obedience" (347).

Notice how Witsius treats our surrender to the lordship of Christ not as a subsequent experience to saving faith but as part of what faith is. He does this by preserving faith as "peculiarly a receiving grace" (to use Andrew Fuller's phrase). That is, he insists that saving faith *receives* "the whole Christ," that is, Christ "just as he is." And "he is no less Lord than a Savior." Hence, surrendering to Christ in this sense is therefore a *receiving* of Christ the Lord. Which means it is part of saving faith—the peculiarly receiving grace.

8. Witsius concludes his description of saving faith, just as Turretin did, with an element of faith that he describes as the *reflex* of the soul looking back on all the other aspects of faith that God has brought about. The function of this reflexive

act is to experience inferentially the confidence that the soul truly does belong to Christ. "After the believing soul has . . . received Christ, and given himself up to him, he may and ought thence to conclude that Christ, with all his saving benefits, [is his]" (347).

Owen: Preferring Christ before All Beloveds

John Owen (1616–1683) may be the greatest theologian in the history of the English-speaking world. Some would say greater than Jonathan Edwards. For example, J. I. Packer wrote, "For solidity, profundity, massiveness and majesty in exhibiting from Scripture God's ways with sinful mankind there is no one to touch him."[12] He is certainly among the handful of writers who have deeply shaped my thinking.

Owen makes it clear that when one believes Christ in a saving way, he is *preferring* Christ above all other "beloveds" (meaning all other persons and all our favorite sins and treasures):

The accepting of Christ by the will, as its only husband, Lord, and Saviour . . . is called "receiving" of Christ, John 1:12. . . . This it is to receive the Lord Jesus *in his comeliness and eminency.* Let believers exercise their hearts abundantly unto this thing. . . . Let us receive him *in all his excellencies,* as he bestows himself upon us;—be frequent in thoughts of faith, comparing him with other beloveds . . . and *preferring him before them, counting them all loss and dung in comparison of him.*[13]

---

12 J. I. Packer, *A Quest for Godliness: The Puritan Vision of the Christian Life* (Wheaton, IL: Crossway, 1990), 81.

13 John Owen, *Of Communion with God the Father, Son, and Holy Ghost,* vol. 2, *The Works of John Owen,* ed. William H. Goold (Edinburgh: T&T Clark, n.d.), 58–59; emphasis added.

"Be frequent in *thoughts* of faith." And when faith *thinks* like this, what happens? It *prefers*. In other words, faith is never just a matter of thinking. In faith, *thinking* about Christ moves to *preferring* Christ. So Owen points me toward the dimension of faith that esteems Christ as its greatest treasure.

For Owen, this "preferring" may be called *love*, as Jesus calls it in Matthew 10:37 ("Whoever *loves* father or mother more than me is not worthy of me"). "There can be no faith in Christ where there is no *love* unto him on the account of his mediatory acts. . . . They whose hearts are not deeply *affected* herewith, can never believe in him in a due manner."[14]

Mastricht: "Reception with Delight"

Peter van Mastricht (1630–1706) was professor of Hebrew and theology at the University of Utrecht. What draws me to him are these words from Jonathan Edwards in a 1746 letter to Joseph Bellamy: "Take Mastricht for divinity in general, doctrine, practice, and controversy; or as a universal system of divinity; and it is much better than Turretin or any other book in the world, excepting the Bible, in my opinion."[15]

Like most other Protestant theologians, Mastricht focuses on saving faith as "receiving":

Because several acts coincide in saving faith—knowledge, assent, consent, trust, and so forth—we must observe that one particular act is predominant among them—the act that when present, salvation is present, and when absent, salvation is absent; thus

14 Owen, *Communion with God the Father, Son, and Holy Ghost*, 165; emphasis added.
15 Jonathan Edwards, *Letters and Personal Writings*, ed. George S. Claghorn, vol. 16, *The Works of Jonathan Edwards* (New Haven: Yale University Press, 1998), 217.

the act that is called saving. What act is it then? The text answers, "Receiving," and the apostle gives this his support (Col. 2:5–7; Phil. 3:8–9, 12; Gal. 4:14; cf. Matt. 26:26).[16]

Then he asks what it means to "receive Christ." His answer is that it "denotes desiring and reception with delight, and disregard for others."[17] This "desiring" is

in the way that a bride receives a bridegroom . . . assenting to him as he offers himself. . . . That is, (1) desiring absolutely, without any condition or restriction, (2) desiring Christ himself, not only his benefits . . . , (3) desiring Christ entirely, not only as Priest or Redeemer, but also as King, as Lord, in the way he is given to us by God. And (4) not only him entirely but also him exclusively, that is, conjugally; (5) not only as a king but also as a servant—not only his glory but also his misery. Finally, (6) desiring him on those terms and conditions by which he offers himself, that is, under the condition of the denial of one's very self, and so forth.[18]

"Reception with delight." This is a strong statement of the affectional dimension of saving faith. Along with the other Protestant theologians cited here, Mastricht shows that defining saving faith as "receiving Christ" does not settle the issue of what saving faith is, because one can receive Christ with so many different states of heart. So Mastricht, with all these Protestant voices, presses us to

16 Petrus van Mastricht, *Faith in the Triune God*, ed. Joel R. Beeke, trans. Todd M. Rester and Michael T. Spangler, vol. 2, Theoretical-Practical Theology (Grand Rapids, MI: Reformation Heritage, 2019), 8–9.
17 Petrus van Mastricht, *Faith in the Triune God*, 9.
18 Petrus van Mastricht, *Faith in the Triune God*, 9.

go to the Scriptures and see not only *that* we should receive Christ, but *how*. He and others press the issue: What is it to receive Christ as a treasure, as living water, as bread from heaven?

Edwards: "Love Is the Main Thing in Saving Faith"

Jonathan Edwards (1703–1758), New England pastor and theologian, was no copycat—not with regard to Mastricht or anyone else. In fact, if anything, he sometimes got himself in trouble by being a bit too independent and idiosyncratic in his views. Whether that is the case with his understanding of saving faith, we will test in due time.

But for now, I will just say that few statements have arrested my attention with a greater sense of urgency than this comment from Edwards's exegesis of 1 John 5:1–4: "Love [to God] is the main thing in saving faith." The main thing! Really? Edwards is not the kind of thinker that we can dismiss easily. So I will return to this when we deal with that passage in 1 John.[19]

Machen: Pushing Back

I close this section on historic Protestant voices with a contrary voice. Up till now, I have pointed to voices that, one way or another, suggest that there is an affectional element in saving faith. They have assumed that this does not undermine the Reformed doctrine of justification by faith alone. But J. Gresham Machen (1881–1937), professor of New Testament at Princeton and Westminster seminaries, sounds a dissenting note and warning.

He asks why the New Testament speaks so pervasively about faith, rather than love, as the doorway to salvation. He answers:

19 See chap. 19.

The true reason why faith is given such an exclusive place by the New Testament, so far as the attainment of salvation is concerned, over against love and over against everything else in man except things that can be regarded as mere aspects of faith [!], is that *faith means receiving something*, not doing something or even being something. To say, therefore, that our faith saves us means that we do not save ourselves even in slightest measure, but that God saves us. Very different would be the case if our salvation were said to be through love; for then salvation would depend upon a high quality of our own. And that is what the New Testament, above all else, is concerned to deny.[20]

I think Machen is right that *faith* is overwhelmingly the New Testament word chosen for our entrance into salvation. And he is right that the main reason for this is that *faith*, better than any other word, draws attention to our being saved by the person and work of another, rather than by our own person or work. He is right to call attention to faith as essentially "receiving"—receiving Christ.

Grudem: A Caution

In our own day, Wayne Grudem, author of the widely used and extremely helpful *Systematic Theology*, shares Machen's concern to keep saving faith distinct from delight in Christ. I have corresponded with him about this issue, and he has given me permission to quote his caution:

The one caution that comes to mind is that I would never want to add any element of "works" as necessary for saving faith. I

20 J. Gresham Machen, *What Is Faith?* (Grand Rapids, MI: Eerdmans, 1925), 173, emphasis added.

72

think it is right to argue that saving faith must include faith + repentance, as two sides of the same coin: we turn *from* sin *to* Christ in one and the same action.

But now do we have to say that genuine faith must include faith + repentance + delight in Christ? How can it be distinguished from faith + a little bit of works?

The other thing I want to be careful about concerns the nature of faith. The New Testament emphasizes faith (*pistis*, *pisteuo*) rather than some other attitudes of mind such as joy or delight or peace, and I think this is because of the unique nature of faith as something opposite human effort. It is admitting, "Lord, I am totally unable to save myself. I give up. I rely upon you."

I think that's the point of Romans 4:16: "That is why it depends on faith, in order that the promise may rest on grace." I don't think Paul could say that about delight, or joy, or peacefulness of mind, etc. And I want to be faithful to that New Testament emphasis.[21]

To the Scriptures!

We must regularly remind ourselves that no theologian, including the author of the book you are reading, has the last word about the nature of saving faith. Outside the Bible, we are all fallible. God has appointed teachers in his church (Eph. 4:11; 1 Tim. 3:2; 2 Tim. 2:2, 24; Heb. 5:12), but only his word is infallible. Therefore, to the Scriptures we will go.

---

21 Email to me dated October 30, 2019. This echoes his *Systematic Theology*: "Why did God choose *faith* as the means by which we receive justification? It is apparently because *faith* is the one attitude of heart that is the exact opposite of depending on ourselves." Wayne A. Grudem, *Systematic Theology: An Introduction to Biblical Doctrine* (Grand Rapids, MI: InterVarsity Press, 2004), 730.

What is especially provocative, and what sends me to the Scriptures for discernment, is that so many Reformed thinkers, who cared as much as Machen and Grudem about justification by faith alone, saw the receiving of Christ not as *a totally different thing from* love to Christ,[22] or delight in Christ, or treasuring Christ, but rather as encompassing in itself that very love and delight and treasuring.[23] In other words, saving faith, many would say, is receiving Christ *as loved*, receiving Christ *as enjoyed*, receiving Christ *as treasured*.

The decisive question is, Did they say these kinds of things for biblical reasons? Does the overall picture of saving faith in the Bible incline us to call faith "peculiarly a receiving grace" and then stop? Or do the Scriptures compel us to press into the *nature* of this "receiving"? The existence of this book is my answer. But before we turn to the exegetical parts of the book (parts 2 through 4), there is one recent angle on saving faith that I find especially troubling, namely, the emphasis on faith as *allegiance*, which argues that "saving faith *includes* good deeds."

---

22 When I speak of "love to Christ" like this, I do not mean the practical outworking of the heart's affection in practical good deeds toward others. I simply mean that affectional dimension of the heart's receiving of Christ that can be called love, alongside, and overlapping with, delight and treasuring. See introduction note 4.

23 In quoting Machen and Grudem, I do not want to give the impression that all twentieth-century Reformed voices are reticent about an affectional aspect to the nature of saving faith. For instance, writing about the "third element" in saving faith (in addition to *noticia* and *assensus*), R. C. Sproul writes that fiducia "is usually understood as involving something in addition to the cognitive or purely intellectual element. It involves the volitional and affective elements of human response. It includes an awareness (which is also intellectual and cognitive) of the sweetness and excellence of Christ. It involves a change in us wrought by regeneration, which change includes a change in affection, disposition, inclination, and volition. We now choose Christ. We embrace Christ. We gladly receive Christ." R. C. Sproul, *Justified by Faith Alone* (Wheaton, IL: Crossway, 2010), 4.

6

Does "Saving Allegiance"
Clarify "Saving Faith"?

I INTERACT WITH Matthew Bates in this chapter, first, because his proposal is a contemporary challenge to what I see in Scripture, and, second, because I think the interaction will help you see more clearly what I am arguing for and why. Bates's proposal is this: "I suggest that 'allegiance' is the best term to use when talking about a saving response to the gospel."[1]

Allegiance as a Response to the Kingship of Jesus

Bates is aware that "allegiance" is "not the root meaning" of *pistis* and *pisteuo* (usually translated "faith" and "believe") (66). In fact, he writes:

> It is probable that Paul, Jesus, and others during the New Testament time period had only one basic image-concept in mind

---

1   Matthew Bates, *Gospel Allegiance: What Faith in Jesus Misses for Salvation in Christ* (Grand Rapids, MI: Brazos Press, 2019), 59. Page numbers in parentheses in the text come from this book.

with regard to the *pistis* word family. It was not allegiance per se. What was it? It was trustworthiness (faithfulness) or trust (faith). Study after study has affirmed that such ideas are the core meaning potential for the *pistis* word family. (67)

One can see the close connection between the idea of "faithfulness" and "allegiance." So Bates poses the question, "Why should we think that allegiance is particularly important when the gospel and salvation are in view?" (66). He answers, "When speaking about how to respond to a Messiah or to good news about a king, a *royal frame* is present, so 'allegiance' is the obvious actualization for *pistis*" (68).

What he means by "royal frame" is that faith occurs in a New Testament framework where the *kingship* of Jesus is central. Bates thinks the absence of this emphasis on the kingship of Jesus is a serious flaw in contemporary Christianity. "The largest problem within Christianity today is the exclusion of Jesus's kingship from the gospel" (98).

Protestant Position "Refined"

Bates's book is written to be a corrective. His view is that "Jesus's kingship [is] the most essential gospel fact" (47). "The gospel can best be summarized as 'Jesus now rules as the forgiving king'" (59). He means this to be heard over against the more traditional view. So he protests, "The cross is not presented as the theological center of the gospel in the Bible" (40). Even more provocatively, he says, "Our justification by faith is not part of the gospel. . . . When we begin saying that it *is* the gospel, or even part of the gospel, we seriously distort the Bible's presentation" (37; also 209).[2]

2   When Bates refers to "our justification," it is not clear whether he means by "our" the justification as offered to *us* all in the gospel or John Piper's actual justification sixty-eight

So, with the "royal frame" in place—namely, that "Jesus's king-ship [is] the most essential gospel fact"—he proposes

> that "allegiance" is the best term to use when talking about a saving response to the gospel. This does not mean that faith is simply allegiance. Yet if the gospel can best be summarized as "Jesus now rules as the forgiving king," then the saving response God requires becomes clear. Jesus the King ultimately requires one and only one thing from his subjects: loyalty. In responding to the gospel, we are saved by allegiance alone. (59)

He presents this view as a *refinement* within the Protestant understanding of salvation by faith:

> Protestants are right that we are saved by faith alone. Yet the classic Protestant position must be further refined, for saving good works do not merely follow upon *pistis* in Jesus. They are part of *pistis* as embodied allegiance to Jesus the king. (153)

> Saving faith is loyalty to Jesus as the forgiving king and includes good deeds done through the power of the Holy Spirit. (228)

Pistis Intends External Performances

The summary statement that brings Bates's proposal into direct conflict with the point of this book includes the assertion that *pistis* (faith) is not an inward feeling or emotion. Here's the fuller statement:

---

years ago in Florida. If he means the latter, the point seems gratuitous. Nobody thinks Paul preached John Piper's justification. If the former, then he has truly set himself over against the Protestant tradition and, I would say, the Scriptures.

In the New Testament era, a person would enact faith (*pistis*) toward someone or something else by *outward doing*. *Pistis* predominantly intends external performance rather than inner attitudes or feelings. . . . You act to show *pistis* (fidelity) to your oath. A subject people shows their *pistis* (loyalty) to their overlords by supporting rather than undermining the regime. . . . Emotions or affections often attend *pistis*, so it is impossible to entirely disentangle inward attitude and external behavior. It is safest to say that *pistis* is related to inward feelings and emotions, but is not itself one. In short, as Morgan concludes, "sources of this period have very little interest in the interiority of *pistis/fides*."[3] (153–54)

How We Differ

The book you are reading argues the opposite. Saving faith is indeed interior. Thus, Paul said, "With *the heart* one believes and is justified" (Rom. 10:10). And spiritual affections do not just "attend *pistis*" but are part of its very nature. And it is not true that in the New Testament *pistis* "predominantly intends external performance"; rather, it is the internal divine gift that gives rise to external performance.

Of the many problems I see with Bates's approach and conclusions, I will try to focus my responses on those matters that touch the central concerns of this book. I have four main responses.

1. Kingship and Allegiance Are Too Narrow

First, Bates bases his proposal on the claim that "Jesus's kingship [is] the most essential gospel fact" (47), and on the inference that "'al-

---

3 The sentence in quotation marks is from Teresa Morgan, *Roman Faith and Christian Faith: Pistis and* Fides *in the Early Roman Empire and Early Churches* (Oxford, UK: Oxford University Press, 2017), 29.

legiance' is the best term to use when talking about a saving response to the gospel" (59). One problem with this argument is that it does not follow that, if kingship is "most essential," therefore *allegiance* is the "best term" to use when talking about how to respond savingly.

Let's leave aside the question of *how* essential the kingship of Jesus is and just agree that it is essential. In other words, if Jesus is not King of kings, then there is no gospel, no salvation, no biblical Christianity. Agreed. But it does not follow that *allegiance* is "the best term to use when talking about a saving response to the gospel." It may be a good term sometimes in some contexts. But to call it, in general, the "best term" does not follow.

The reason it doesn't is that Christ, in all of his saving and satisfying greatness, is offered to us as vastly more than a king. He is to be received in a saving way in *all* of his identities. But *allegiance* is not the best term to describe the receiving of Christ in all his roles.

For example, he is offered to us as "Savior" (John 4:42), "Master and Lord" (Jude 1:4), "the power of God and the wisdom of God" (1 Cor. 1:24), "[our] righteousness and sanctification and redemption" (1 Cor. 1:30), "friend" (Luke 7:34), "the hope of glory" (Col. 1:27), "Helper" (John 14:16), "teacher" (John 3:2), "living water" (John 4:10), "bread of life" (John 6:48), "light of the world" (John 8:12), "treasure" (Matt. 13:44), and more.

Try speaking of allegiance to a friend, or allegiance to living water, or allegiance to the bread of heaven, or allegiance to a treasure. I have no objection to the word *allegiance* as a proper demand from Christ's followers. But to elevate the kingship of Jesus the way Bates does obscures the amazing variety of ways in which Christ offers us his saving and satisfying glory. And to call *allegiance* the best term in response to the fullness of Christ, and to give it the sweeping role that Bates does, is not helpful.

Perhaps Bates would respond by pointing out that his approach is to define the *gospel proper* and then define the *best* saving response in relation to that. And kingship is "most essential," he would say, to the gospel proper. Thus allegiance is the "best term" for a saving response to that distinct view of the gospel.

But I think that approach inevitably leads to a misrepresentation of the New Testament message. It is artificial and reductionistic to collect texts marked by the word *gospel* (*euangelion*), find the kingship of Jesus in those texts, foreground kingship as "most essential," and infer that across the entire New Testament "allegiance" (to a king) is "the best" term for a saving response.

The result of this approach is breathtakingly narrow. And using the magnificent words *gospel* and *king* and *allegiance* does not make it less narrow. By *narrow* I mean that it overlooks, and thus mutes, many biblical texts that are relevant to the truth and glory and goodness of life in Christ and how to have it. *Kingship* and *allegiance* are true realities of New Testament revelation. Glorious realities. But great as they are, the scope and variety of New Testament revelation about Christ and the path of our salvation are greater—far greater.

2. Rejecting the Protestant View, Not Refining

A second, and more serious, problem with Bates's approach and conclusions is his claim to be *refining* the historic Protestant understanding of salvation by faith. As it turns out, his proposal is not a refinement but a rejection. Historic Reformation teaching is that faith does not *include* good works, but *bears the fruit* of good works. The Westminster Confession (11.2) says:

Faith, thus receiving and resting on Christ and his righteousness is the sole instrument of justification; yet it is not alone in the person justified, but is ever accompanied with all other saving graces, and is no dead faith, but works by love.

Faith and works are distinct. Works *accompany* saving faith. Saving faith *gives rise* to good works. They are not the same. "Every healthy tree bears good fruit" (Matt. 7:17). So "make the tree good and its fruit good . . . for the tree is known by its fruit" (Matt. 12:33). But you can't pursue good fruit by making a good tree, if the fruit is the tree. But that is what Bates argues:

> The classic Protestant position must be further refined, for *saving good works do not merely follow upon* pistis (faith) *in Jesus. They are part of* pistis *as embodied allegiance* to Jesus the king. (153; emphasis added)

> Saving faith is loyalty to Jesus as the forgiving king and *includes good deeds* done through the power of the Holy Spirit. (228; emphasis added)

This is not a refinement. It is the opposite of what the Reformation taught. And the difference is central. To claim that good works are not the fruit of saving faith but are part of its nature has two destructive effects: it opposes the precious and glorious reality of justification by faith *apart from works* (Rom. 3:28), and it opposes the power provided by faith for obeying Christ. That is, it opposes the kingship of Jesus (see the third response below).

Paul said in Titus 3:5, "[God] saved us, *not because of works done by us in righteousness*, but according to his own mercy." Paul is bent on making clear that our decisive deliverance from the guilt and power of sin and Satan and death, as we come into union with Christ, is not owing to deeds done by us in righteousness. Bates wants to persuade us that saving faith (that is, allegiance), "includes good deeds done through the power of the Holy Spirit," and that "we are united to him through allegiance" (74). Paul, on the other hand, wants to turn all our attention away from "deeds done by us in righteousness" and fix our dependence entirely on the mercy of God.

Paul's words in Galatians 5:2–4 are even more emphatic about excluding the smallest good work from our dependence on grace:

> Look: I, Paul, say to you that if you accept circumcision, Christ will be of no advantage to you. I testify again to every man who accepts circumcision that he is obligated to keep the whole law. You are severed from Christ, you who would be justified by the law; you have fallen away from grace.

The point here is this: if you mingle with faith one little outward act of law-keeping as part of your pathway into right standing with God, you are obliged to keep the whole law. You either stand accepted and right with God by grace through faith alone, or you stand accepted and right with God through perfect law-keeping.

And Paul has already ruled out the second option: "We know that a person is not justified by works of the law but through faith in Jesus Christ" (Gal. 2:16).[4] Justification by good deeds (even good deeds that call themselves "allegiance") will never happen. And everyone who tries it is under a curse. "All who rely on works

---

4   If you are inclined to follow the New Perspective on Paul and thus think that "works of the law" (in Gal. 2:16) is limited to ceremonial boundary markers of Jewishness and irrelevant for making my point, I would refer you not only to the argument here, but also to Stephen Westerholm, *Justification Reconsidered* (Grand Rapids, MI: Eerdmans, 2013), especially chap. 5, "Not by Works of the Law."

of the law are under a curse; for it is written, 'Cursed be everyone who does not abide by all things written in the Book of the Law, and do them'" (Gal. 3:10). Either we keep perfectly "all things" written in the law, or we bow to justification by faith alone, apart from any good deeds.

In trying to make good deeds "part of *pistis*" (faith), Bates opposes the biblical reality of justification by faith alone apart from works. If this sounds familiar, it may be because this is similar to the mistake made by the Roman Catholicism of the Council of Trent. We saw in chapter 3 that Roman Catholicism conflates saving faith and the virtuousness of sanctification: "Faith, unless hope and charity be added thereto, neither unites man perfectly with Christ, nor makes him a living member of His body" (Council of Trent in the Decree on Justification, chapter 7). Bates is a Protestant, but he admits explicitly that when he teaches that "we are saved by allegiance . . . it smells Catholic" (21).

3. Irony of Undermining Obedient Allegiance to the King

Third, and perhaps most ironically, in conflating faith and works, Bates opposes the power provided by faith for obeying Christ. That is, his way of treating allegiance to Jesus's kingship undermines the very power of obedient allegiance to the king.

Bates does not want to distinguish faith as an interior act of the heart from external holy behavior that results from it. Rather, he insists that "saving good works do not merely follow upon *pistis* (faith) in Jesus. They are part of *pistis*" (153). "Saving faith . . . includes good deeds" (228).

This conflation at best obscures, and at worst severs, the vital causal connection between the root of faith and the fruit of love. Paul teaches that faith is internal. It is an act of the heart, not the body. We are to "believe *in [our] heart* that God raised [Jesus] from the dead. . . . For *with the heart one believes* and is justified" (Rom. 10:9–10). This interior miraculous work of the Spirit is the vital source of power by which we love others. "The aim of our charge is *love* that issues from a pure heart and a good conscience and a sincere *faith*" (1 Tim. 1:5). Faith does not include love for others. Faith issues in love. To turn the root into the fruit destroys the source of the fruit.

For Paul, faith is the great means by which the Holy Spirit produces his fruit. "Does he who supplies the Spirit to you and works miracles among you do so by works of the law, or by hearing with faith?" (Gal. 3:5). Faith is the great power that issues in works of love. "In Christ Jesus neither circumcision nor uncircumcision counts for anything, but only faith working through love" (Gal. 5:6). The kind of faith that justifies produces the works of love. But they are not the same.

"*By faith* Abraham obeyed" (Heb. 11:8). The obedience was not the faith. It came *by* faith. So Paul says, "The life I now live in the flesh I live *by faith* in the Son of God" (Gal. 2:20). His living is not his faith. He lived *by* his faith. By conflating faith and allegiance, and then defining allegiance to include good works, Bates cuts off the New Testament path of holiness.

That path begins with the instantaneous act of justification by faith alone, apart from works. Then, on the basis of our acceptance and right standing with God, we are able with hope to put to death the old nature and walk in holiness. The uniqueness and the glory of the New Testament path of sanctification, and the power to kill sin (Rom. 8:13), is that this path is walked, and this warfare is fought, by those who have been once for all justified by faith alone. If our lives of holiness are equated with the faith by which we are united to Christ and justified, we no longer are able to strive for holiness as accepted and forgiven children of God. Rather, we will always be striving to be accepted and forgiven, since justifying faith and lives of holiness have been merged. That is why the unique, glorious New Testament way of following King Jesus is undermined by the teaching of Matthew Bates.

4. Interiority and Affectional Nature of Saving Faith?

Fourth, the point at which Bates's view of saving faith conflicts most directly with what I am arguing for in this book is his contention that the New Testament has "very little interest in the interiority of *pistis/fides*" (154).[5] Affections only "attend *pistis*"; they are not part of what *pistis* is. "It is safest to say that *pistis* is related to inward feelings and emotions, but is not itself one" (154).

Like the other issues in part 1 of this book, this issue about the affectional nature of saving faith launches us into the rest of this book. The book is my answer to this claim. I am arguing that there are indeed affectional elements in saving faith, and the "interiority of *pistis*" (the life of the heart!) is of great importance in the New Testament. It is not marginal.

Allegiance Is Indeed Essential

I do not discount or diminish the importance of real allegiance to King Jesus. No one will be saved without it. If I were to describe it as an essential element of saving faith, by which we come into union with Christ, which I am willing to do, my definition would be radically different from Bates's definition. I would not define it to include good deeds. I would say that, as part of saving faith,

5   Again, Bates quotes this from Morgan, *Roman Faith and Christian Faith*, 29.

allegiance is a *glad receiving of Jesus as King* with all that this implies for life and eternity. Of course, no new believer knows all the implications. But saving faith happily welcomes the truth it knows with the implications it can see. If the faith is real, the rest of eternity will reveal more and more of the glories of the king, with an ever-expanding welcome in the heart of the believer.

PART 2

SEEING REALITY THROUGH
SIX HUNDRED LENSES

So far I have taken for granted that I share with the reader a general sense about the meaning of *faith*. So I have not paused to define it. I have posed the question about whether saving faith includes spiritual affections, as if I could assume we shared a meaning for "faith" in general. But now we need to step back and let the Scriptures themselves define faith in a general sense (part 2). Then we can be more specific and look at texts that point to the affectional content of saving faith (indirectly in part 3 and directly in part 4).

Defining Faith Biblically: Three Ways

How shall we go about defining faith biblically? Before I explain what I mean by "six hundred lenses," let me mention three ways that I will approach defining faith *biblically*.

1. New Testament Focus

First, I am going to focus on the New Testament. This is not because saving faith is missing from the Old Testament. In fact, Paul builds his case for justification by faith on Genesis 15:6: "What does the Scripture say? 'Abraham *believed* God, and it was counted to him as righteousness'" (Rom. 4:3). The reason for focusing on the New Testament is, first, to keep the book shorter, and, second, because the fullest and final treatment of saving faith is in the New Testament. If we see matters accurately in the New Testament, we will be true to God's aims in the Old Testament.

2. Meaning as a Shared General Sense

Second, the meaning of a word assumes a mean-er, one who does the meaning. Whenever we say, "Faith means such and such," we are claiming to understand what some person, or persons, means. This is important because different authors may use the same word in different ways. Jesus might say, "Your faith has saved you" (Luke 7:50). And James might ask skeptically, "Can that faith save him?" (James 2:14). These are not contradictory views of reality. But they are different uses of the word *faith*.

Not only that, but even the same author can use the same word with different meanings at different times (as we all do from time to time: "As I rock in my chair, the rock music from next door, shatters my peace like a rock thrown through a glass window."). In the second chapter of his letter, James refers to "faith" that is "dead" (James 2:17, 26) and cannot save (v. 14). But in chapter 5, he refers to faith that is very much alive and "has great power as it is working" (5:16, and does indeed save, v. 15).

So, as I try to define faith biblically, I realize that all precise definitions depend on specific contexts that reveal the particular intentions of an author. Nevertheless, it is possible to be less precise and to speak of a more general intention—a more general definition—that multiple authors (and multiple groups) share. Without this, even the specific meanings that authors give to a word would not be possible. Authors always start with some shared assumptions about their words, and then they give them their own specific sense. For now, this set of shared assumptions—this broader, general meaning of faith—is what I am looking for among the New Testament authors.

3. Aiming at Experienced Reality

Third, my aim in defining a biblical term is that we *experience* the reality it represents the way the inspired writers want us to. I am not content to replace one word (say, *faith*) with some other words (say, *trust* and *confidence*), call it a definition, and say my work is done. My goal, for myself and others, in all my Bible reading and teaching and writing is to penetrate through language to the *reality* that words represent. If the Bible says, "Trust in the LORD" (Prov. 3:5), my aim is not only to interpret the word *trust* with a new set of words, like, "Experience peaceful confidence as you rest in the Lord's promises." My aim is that we *experience* in our minds and hearts and actions all that the inspired author intends for us to experience.[1]

Words and the realities they signify are not the same. The word *kiss* is not a kiss. The word *happiness* is not happiness. The word

---

1   See John Piper, *Reading the Bible Supernaturally* (Wheaton, IL: Crossway, 2017), 301, where I discuss the author's intention as including his intention that we not just understand what he is saying, but experience it.

faith or *believe* is not the experiential reality required for salvation. Words are pointers. They point to realities other than themselves. This is why we begin with an effort to clarify the general meaning of faith in the New Testament, but we will move (in parts 3 and 4) inevitably toward the affectional realities that the authors seek to communicate. We find and experience those realities not only by clarifying the general meaning of *faith*, but also by watching carefully how the authors reveal the peculiar dimensions that the word, by itself, does not make clear.

Six Hundred Lenses

The title of part 2 is "Seeing Reality through Six Hundred Lenses." By "six hundred lenses," I am referring to the 602 words in the New Testament built from the stem of the Greek word for *faith* or *believe*, the stem πιστ- (*pist-*). If you look up all the uses of the words *believe* and *faith* in an English New Testament, virtually all of them will be a translation of some form of the Greek stem *pist-*.

So this is where my focus will be. I have tried to process all six hundred of these uses and will attempt to distill what I found into nine steps of clarification for the general meaning of *saving faith*. When I refer to the general meaning of *saving faith*, I also have in mind both *saving belief* and *saving believing*, since *faith* and *belief* (or *believe*) are built on the same stem in Greek, unlike in English. As these nine steps of clarification progress, I don't mean that each step *by itself* would be saving faith. Rather, I mean that each of these clarifications, in conjunction with the others, is an element of saving faith.

I do not focus in part 2 on the affectional nature of saving faith. That comes especially in part 4. Part 2 lays the more general foundation. It is an attempt to answer, What are we assuming about the term *saving faith* in a *general sense*, when we ask, "Does *saving faith* have an affectional dimension?" In chapter 7, we will focus on the first four clarifications about saving faith, since they are relatively brief. Then in chapters 8 through 12, we will devote a chapter to each of the last five clarifications, since they are more lengthy.

7

Confident Trust in What Jesus Says

(Clarifications 1–4)

Clarification 1

Saving faith refers to regarding someone's words as true and reliable, and thus recognizing that the reality he speaks of is true and real. Thus his words are received as reliable.

We see this aspect of faith in the following texts and many others:

- The angel Gabriel said to Zechariah, "Behold, you will be silent and unable to speak until the day that these things take place, because you did not believe my words" (Luke 1:20).

- On the contrary, Mary did credit the words of the angel as true. So Elizabeth said to her, "Blessed is she who believed that there would be a fulfillment of what was spoken to her from the Lord" (Luke 1:45).

- Jesus said to the official whose son was dying, "'Go; your son will live.' The man believed the word that Jesus spoke to him and went on his way" (John 4:50).

- Jesus said to Philip, "Do you not believe that I am in the Father and the Father is in me? The words that I say to you I do not speak on my own authority, but the Father who dwells in me does his works" (John 14:10).

This idea of "regarding as true" can be described in different ways. One could say, "We *give* the words credence." Or one could say, "We *receive* the words as credible." Notice that one way of saying it calls attention to what we *give* (credence), and the other way of saying it calls attention to what we *receive* (credible words). This is why the nature of saving faith will never be settled simply by focusing on the definitions of biblical words for *faith*. Words for *faith* can be taken in too many different ways.

Significantly, Jesus said, "I have given them the words that you [Father] gave me, and they have *received* them and have come to know in truth that I came from you; and they have *believed* that you sent me" (John 17:8). Jesus draws attention to our "receiving" his words, and thus coming to know and "believe" that he is from God. This fits with a pattern we will see: that even though believing is indeed an act of *regarding as true*, the truth is not *in us*, but is outside of us and must be *received as true*. In a sense, the *act* of faith is a *being acted upon*. When we *regard as true*, we are being acted upon by the reality we regard: it shows itself firm and reliable to our minds and hearts. We do not create the reality that we "give credence" to. It exists independently of us. We *receive* it as real and reliable.[1]

---

1   This is confirmed by the striking way the Greek Old Testament (LXX) uses the Greek word for believe, πιστεύω (*pisteuō*). *Pisteuō* occurs some forty-six times in the LXX (when the apocryphal

Clarification 2

Saving faith is the kind of experience that is contrary to doubt.

I use the phrase "contrary to doubt" rather than "the opposite of doubt" because faith often battles with doubt rather than completely excluding it:

As he stood on the water, while Peter and the others were in the boat, Jesus said to Peter, "'Come.' So Peter got out of the boat

---

books are omitted). Surprisingly, it never translates the most common verb for *trust* in the Hebrew OT, בטח (*batah*), which is used some 116 times—translated roughly half of the time with ἐλπίζω (*elpizo*, I hope) and half with *peithō* (πείθω, I persuade). Rather, *pisteuō* is always (some 46 times) a translation of the Hiphil verb form of אמן (*'aman*), which has the basic thrust of "be reliable, firm, real." That strikes me as amazing—that the most common verb for *trust* in the Greek Old Testament is *never* translated by the most common New Testament word for believe (πιστεύω)! What does it mean for the use of πιστεύω in the New Testament?

My suggestion is this: *batah* foregrounds the inner state of confidence in the one who trusts. But the Hiphil of *'aman* (translated by πιστεύω) foregrounds the acknowledgment of firmness and truth and reality in the one being believed (the Hiphil having not a causative sense, but one of crediting). Nevertheless, it would be a mistake to think that trust (*batah*) has no connotations of the truth, firmness, and reality of what is trusted. Likewise, it would be a mistake to think that believing (Hiphil of *'aman*) has no connotation of inner trust and confidence. In fact, these are almost interchangeable in texts like Ps. 78:22 ("They did not *believe* [הֶאֱמִינוּ] in God and did not *trust* [בָטְחוּ] his saving power") and Mic. 7:5 ("Put no trust in [תַּאֲמִינוּ] a neighbor; have no confidence in [תִּבְטְחוּ] a friend").

Thus, in reality, both words include both an acknowledgment of reliable reality *and* a conscious experience of confidence. But the Hiphil of *'aman* seems to begin with the firmness of the object and then move forward to the experience of trust, while *batah* seems to begin with the experience of trust and move backward toward the firmness of the one trusted. Thus, by translating the Hiphil of *'aman* with *pisteuō*, the LXX translators suggest that the *pisteuō* word carries for them that implication: credit the firmness of a source and then, in various ways, show implications of trust and confidence. Artur Weiser points in this same direction in the OT half of the article on *pisteuō* in TDNT: "בטח here means 'to be in a state of security' (בָּטַח). . . . Even where בְּ, עַל or אֶל is added to denote the author or means of security, בטח in distinction from הֶאֱמִן expresses the state rather than the relation, so that the translation [of הֶאֱמִן as], 'to feel secure on the basis of . . .' is nearest the mark." Rudolf Bultmann and Artur Weiser, πιστεύω, *Theological Dictionary of the New Testament*, ed. Gerhard Kittel, Geoffrey W. Bromiley, and Gerhard Friedrich (Grand Rapids, MI: Eerdmans, 1964–), 6:191.

and walked on the water and came to Jesus. But when he saw the wind, he was afraid, and beginning to sink he cried out, 'Lord, save me.' Jesus immediately reached out his hand and took hold of him, saying to him, 'O you of little *faith*, why did you *doubt*?'" (Matt. 14:29–31).

Jesus said to his disciples, "Truly, I say to you, if you *have faith* and *do not doubt*, you will not only do what has been done to the fig tree, but even if you say to this mountain, 'Be taken up and thrown into the sea,' it will happen" (Matt. 21:21).

James writes, "Let him ask *in faith*, with *no doubting*, for the one who doubts is like a wave of the sea that is driven and tossed by the wind" (James 1:6).

The point I am drawing attention to here is that faith is an inner experience that is contrary to doubt. I'm not even trying to name that experience here (confidence?); I'm only emphasizing what some have denied[2]—namely, that faith is an interior state of the soul, like doubt is, only it is contrary to doubt.

Clarification 3

Saving faith is a kind of experience that is contrary to anxiety and fear.

---

2   Teresa Morgan, *Roman Faith and Christian Faith:* Pistis *and* Fides *in the Early Roman Empire and Early Churches* (Oxford, UK: Oxford University Press, 2017), 154, claims that "sources of this period have very little interest in the interiority of *pistis/fides*." When one thinks of the vastness of the "period" she is dealing with, and the vastness of the "empire," and the vastness of the variety of writers and writings and situations and literary contexts, such a generalization cannot prove helpful when making concrete observations of specific texts. In the New Testament, it simply cannot stand up.

As with the preceding clarification, I use the phrase "contrary to anxiety" rather than "opposite to anxiety" to leave room for the biblical fact that faith may be in conflict with anxiety without ceasing to be saving faith:

> Jesus said, "If God so clothes the grass of the field, which today is alive and tomorrow is thrown into the oven, will he not much more clothe you, O you of *little faith*? Therefore *do not be anxious*" (Matt. 6:30–31).

> Jesus said to them, "'Why are you *afraid*, O you of *little faith*?' Then he rose and rebuked the winds and the sea, and there was a great calm" (Matt. 8:26).

> The author of Hebrews writes, "By *faith* [Moses] left Egypt, *not being afraid* of the anger of the king, for he endured as seeing him who is invisible" (Heb. 11:27).

It is illuminating to consider that faith runs contrary not only to doubt (clarification 2) but also to fear. It illumines the fact that faith manifests differing aspects of its nature as it is challenged by differing experiences of the soul. The experience that is contrary to doubt is not exactly the same as the experience that is contrary to fear. Thus, faith shows one aspect of its nature in the presence of doubt and another aspect of its nature in the presence of fear. Over against doubt, faith is an experience like confidence, conviction, certainty. Over against fear, faith is an experience like a sense of security and peace.

You might say that I am getting ahead of myself here, because I am implying that these affectional states, like confidence and peacefulness, are part of what faith *is*, when others might say that these affectional states are only the *effect and fruit* of faith, not part of its nature. You are right. I have gotten ahead of myself. It's hard to keep hidden what I consider so clear. But if you need more exegetical argument, it is coming.

For now, to help you keep an open mind, consider what it would imply about the meaning of saving faith if it were reduced to a bare mental assent with no heartfelt confidence before God, no peacefulness before the condemnation of the law, no sense of security before the threat of hell. Are we really able to distinguish such affectional experiences from saving faith? What would be the effect of trying to distinguish *faith* or *trust* from such heartfelt confidence, and such peacefulness, and such a sense of security? Would not the effect be to leave the term *faith* or *trust* with no useful meaning? That's where my argument will lead in parts 3 and 4. But even now, I commend it to your biblically informed, intuitive judgment.

Clarification 4

Saving faith is not simply a confident trust in general in Jesus and God the Father, but more specifically that they can and will do what they say.

It is possible to have a general sense of trust in people because of their good character without feeling confident that they can and will do exactly what they say. But faith in Jesus, and what God is for us in him, includes this specific confidence. Consider just two examples of this point, one from Jesus and one from Paul:

The centurion replied, "Lord, I am not worthy to have you come under my roof, but only say the word, and my servant will be healed." . . . When Jesus heard this, he marveled and said to those who followed him, "Truly, I tell you, with no one in Israel have I found such *faith*." . . . And to the centurion Jesus said, "Go; let it be done for you as you have *believed*." And the servant was healed at that very moment. (Matt. 8:8–13)

In hope [Abraham] *believed* against hope, that he should become the father of many nations, as he had been told, "So shall your offspring be." He did not weaken in *faith* when he considered his own body, which was as good as dead (since he was about a hundred years old), or when he considered the barrenness of Sarah's womb. No *unbelief* made him waver concerning the promise of God, but he grew strong in his *faith* as he gave glory to God. (Rom. 4:18–20)

The centurion said, in effect, "Though my servant is paralyzed beyond human help, if you, Jesus, say the word, my servant will be healed." He is confident of it. Abraham said, in effect, "Though I am old and my wife is barren, God's promise of offspring will come true for us." He is confident of it. This confidence is rooted in the words of God. They will come true. Saving faith is like this. It is not simply confidence in general. It is a confident trust rooted specifically in God's and Jesus's reliability.

8

Saving Faith Receives Christ Himself

(Clarification 5)

Clarification 5

Saving faith goes beyond confidence in Christ's reliability, and receives him—not just his word, but himself, that is, all that God is for us in him.

The seminal text that connects believing in Christ with receiving Christ is John 1:11–13:

> [Jesus] came to his own, and his own people did not *receive* him. But to all who did *receive* him, who *believed* in his name, he gave the right to become children of God, who were born, not of blood nor of the will of the flesh nor of the will of man, but of God.

John puts *believing* in Jesus's name in apposition with *receiving* him. "All who did *receive* him, [that is,] who *believed* in his name . . ." *Receiving* Jesus is one way of describing *believing* in Jesus in a saving way.

To Receive the Son Is to Have the Father, and Life

Since Jesus and the Father are one (John 10:30), receiving Jesus includes receiving the Father. This truth lay behind Jesus's statement, "I have come *in my Father's name*, and you do not *receive* me" (John 5:43). Receiving Jesus "in the Father's name" means that when we receive him, we receive the Father and all that he is for us in Jesus. "Whoever receives me receives *the one who sent me*" (John 13:20; cf. Matt. 10:40). A saving relationship with the Father hangs on receiving Jesus.

Receiving Jesus is saving because "as the Father has life in himself, so he has granted the Son also to have life in himself" (John 5:26). Therefore, "Whoever has the Son has life; whoever does not have the Son of God does not have life" (1 John 5:12). Receiving the Son is how we "have" the Son. And only by having the Son do we have life. Indeed, only by "receiving" and thus "having" the Son do we have all that the Father is for us in the Son. Therefore, *saving faith* (John 1:12) is a *receiving* of Jesus Christ and all that God is for us in him.

"You Received Christ Jesus the Lord"

Not only John and Jesus, but also Paul connects "receiving" Jesus with faith: "As you *received* Christ Jesus the Lord, so walk in him, rooted and built up in him and established in the *faith*, just as you were taught, abounding in thanksgiving" (Col. 2:6–7). As we "receive" Christ, so he dwells in us. Thus, Christ's indwelling is "through faith." So Paul prays that "Christ may dwell in your hearts *through faith*" (Eph. 3:17).

All believers, Paul says, have received Christ so that he dwells in them by his Spirit: "Anyone who does not have the Spirit of Christ does not belong to him. But if *Christ is in you*, although the body is dead because of sin, the Spirit is life because of righteousness" (Rom. 8:9–10).

Thus, Christ is "in" every believer. He is there *by faith*: "It is no longer I who live, but Christ who lives in me. And the life I now live in the flesh I live *by faith* in the Son of God, who loved me and gave himself for me" (Gal. 2:20). "By faith" in God's Son, he dwells in us. So saving faith is both the *first* receiving of Christ (John 1:12; Col. 2:6), and the *ongoing* spirit of glad welcome to him and dependence on him hour by hour (Gal. 2:20; Eph. 3:17).

The *receiving* nature of saving faith colors every aspect of the Christian life—interior and exterior. The good that we experience *inwardly* is always a kind of receiving. Thus, Hebrews 13:21 says that God is "working in us that which is pleasing in his sight." God gives; we receive. Similarly, the good we are able to do outwardly is always a kind of receiving. Thus, Paul says, "I worked harder than any of them, though it was not I, but the grace of God that is with me" (1 Cor. 15:10)—a grace *received* by faith. Inward or outward, the life of faith is a life of receiving. "What do you have that you did not receive?" (1 Cor. 4:7).

All Saving Faith Is Receiving Jesus Christ

This must be emphasized. To believe savingly is to *receive* and *have* Jesus Christ. When Paul preached the "gospel of . . . salvation" (Eph. 1:13)—that is, the "gospel of the grace of God" (Acts 20:24)—he preached "the unsearchable riches of Christ" (Eph. 3:8). To receive salvation is to receive Christ and all the unsearchable riches that God is for us in him.

In union with Christ, he becomes for us "wisdom from God, righteousness and sanctification and redemption" (1 Cor. 1:30). Saving faith is *receiving* Christ, not just his gifts, because only in union with Christ, by his indwelling, does all salvation flow to us. God "has blessed us *in Christ* with every spiritual blessing in the heavenly places" (Eph. 1:3). It can scarcely be overemphasized that all saving faith is *receiving*—that is, receiving the person Jesus Christ.

9

The Spiritual Sight of the Glory of Christ

(Clarification 6)

Clarification 6

Saving faith includes spiritual sight of reality, especially a sight of the self-authenticating glory of Christ.

Walking by Faith, Not by Sight

When speaking of the fact that Jesus, in his physical body, is now in heaven while we are still on the earth, Paul said, "We are always of good courage. We know that while we are at home in the body we are away from the Lord, for *we walk by faith, not by sight*" (2 Cor. 5:6–7).[1] What does this imply about walking by faith?

---

1   The words translated, "We walk by faith, not by *sight*" (2 Cor. 5:7) could be rendered literally, "We walk by faith and not by *appearance*," that is, not by what is seen (see the use of εἴδους in 1 Thess. 5:22, "every *form* of evil"). But it comes to the same thing: walking by appearance means walking by how physical things *appear* to our physical *sight*.

Paul does not mean that when we have faith we cease to use our physical eyes to keep from running into walls and falling down stairs. We still "walk by sight" in that sense. He means we cease to use our physical eyes to see Christ. We do not use our physical eyes to discern the truths about Christ that sustain us and guide us. Christ is in heaven. We cannot see him with physical eyes. In that sense, we walk by faith, not by sight.

If walking "by faith" means we don't even walk by *spiritual* sight, or *any* sight at all, then walking by faith doesn't provide a suitable alternative to walking by (physical) sight. For example, if I say, "We don't walk by the physical sight of Christ, but by trust in Christ," the contrast is confusing. The disciples already trusted in Christ while they could see him with physical eyes. And we will have trust in Christ when we *see* him at his coming (1 John 3:1–2). So to contrast walking by sight with walking by trust is not to the point. It's not a real contrast. The most natural contrast in 2 Corinthians 5:7 is between "not by sight" (with the physical eyes) but by another kind of sight, namely, the kind that is part of saving faith.

Thus to make the best sense of the contrast (not by physical sight but by faith) we should take "by faith" to include *a different kind of sight.* So I am suggesting that when Paul says, "We walk by faith, not by sight," he means, "We are sustained and guided by a spiritual sight of Christ, not by a physical sight of Christ."

No Longer Blind to the Light of the Glory of Christ

There are good reasons to think that Paul and other New Testament writers understood saving faith as a kind of spiritual sight of spiritual reality, especially the self-authenticating glory of Christ. For example, Paul contrasts believers and unbelievers by what they see and don't see in the gospel of the glory of Christ:

If our gospel is veiled, it is veiled to those who are perishing. In their case the god of this world has blinded the minds of the *unbelievers*, to keep them from seeing the light of the gospel of the glory of Christ, who is the image of God. . . . For God, who said, "Let light shine out of darkness," has shone in our hearts to give the light of the knowledge of the glory of God in the face of Jesus Christ. (2 Cor. 4:3–6)

Unbelievers are blind to "the light of the gospel of the glory of Christ." But for believers, "God . . . has shone in our hearts" to give that very light. Both groups hear the gospel story. Both grasp the historical facts of the gospel. But unbelievers can't see what believers see in the gospel. Unbelievers are still walking by (natural) sight, not by faith. And natural sight looks at the gospel with no spiritual awareness of the glory of Christ in it. The natural mind (1 Cor. 2:14), with its natural eyes, does not see what faith sees in the gospel.

But the case is very different with believers. They are described in verse 6. They experience the miracle of God's light-giving new creation. They see what unbelievers do not see. God said, as on the first day of creation, "Let there be light!" And by that faith-creating word, God gives "the light of the knowledge of the glory of God in the face of Jesus Christ" (2 Cor. 4:6). When this happens, unbelievers become believers. This is the grand and fundamental difference between believers and unbelievers. Hearing the gospel, *believers see the glory of God* in the face of Christ.

It is a spiritual sight, not a physical one. It is a seeing with what Paul calls "the eyes of the heart." When Paul prays in Ephesians 1:18 that the *eyes of our hearts* would be "enlightened" (πεφωτισμένους, *pephōtismenous*), it is the verb form of the very word used in

2 Corinthians 4:4 and 6 to refer to the God-given "light" (φωτι-σμὸν, *phōtismon*) of Christ's glory. Therefore, I infer that believers have the gift of spiritual sight of spiritual reality, especially the glory of Christ.

As Seeing the Unseen

The writer to the Hebrews also connects faith with the power to see what is unseen: "By faith [Moses] . . . endured *as seeing him who is invisible*" (τὸν ἀόρατον ὡς ὁρῶν ἐκαρτέρησεν, *ton aoraton hōs horōn ekarterēsen*, Heb. 11:27). He says "as" seeing the unseen, not because it wasn't a real kind of seeing, but because it was "as" *physical* seeing. It was a *spiritual* seeing. He "looked" to the invisible Christ (v. 26), as we ourselves are told to do in Hebrews 12:2, even though Christ is invisible to us on earth: ". . . *looking* to Jesus, the founder and perfecter of our faith." We see Christ, by faith, though he is in heaven. It is the same as what believers do in 2 Corinthians 4:18: "We look not to the things that are seen but to the things that are unseen." We look. And we see the unseen.

Moses's seeing "by faith" (Heb. 11:27) connects back to the beginning of Hebrews 11: "Now faith is the assurance of things hoped for, the conviction of *things not seen*" (v. 1). I will say more on this verse in chapters 10 and 17, but for now, I only observe that the writer to the Hebrews joins Paul in the conviction that, by faith, we see the (physically) unseen, most importantly the glory of Christ.

Not Seeing, but Believing, You Rejoice

I mention one more pointer to faith as a kind of spiritual seeing. Peter says in 1 Peter 1:8, "Though you have not seen him, you love him. Though you do not now see him, you *believe* in him and rejoice with joy that is inexpressible and filled with glory." These believers do not see Christ now and have never seen him in their lives—that is, with their physical eyes. Yet they love him, and they rejoice in him with inexpressible and glory-permeated joy.

The last part of verse 8 says, literally, "in whom, while not seeing, but believing, you rejoice" (εἰς ὃν ἄρτι μὴ ὁρῶντες, πιστεύοντες δὲ, ἀγαλλιᾶσθε, *eis hon arti mē horōntes, pisteuontes de, agalliasthe*). To use the language of the apostle Paul from 2 Corinthians 5:7, we could say, "They rejoiced by faith, not by sight," which I am suggesting means this: the support for this unspeakable joy, which would ordinarily be provided by physical sight of Christ, is replaced by spiritual sight of Christ, that is, by faith.

Seeing Self-Authenticating Glory

In sum, then, this sixth clarification is that saving faith includes spiritual sight of spiritual reality, especially the self-authenticating glory of Christ. There are two reasons why I say that faith sees *especially the self-authenticating glory of Christ.*

First, Paul mentions explicitly in 2 Corinthians 4:4, 6 "the glory of Christ, who is the image of God" and "the glory of God in the face of Jesus Christ." This is what unbelievers cannot see and what believers do see when God creates light in their hearts and they fix the eyes of their hearts on the story of the gospel.

Second, I call this glory "self-authenticating" because 2 Corinthians 4:6 describes it as a glory recognized instantaneously by the creative act of God. "God, who said, 'Let light shine out of darkness,' has shone in our hearts to give the light of the knowledge of the glory of God in the face of Jesus Christ." When God causes his glory to shine in our hearts, we do not have the option of finding it either glorious or boring. If we find the glory in verse 6 boring, then we have not yet experienced the miracle of verse 6. We are still in the blindness of verse 4. The point of verse 6 is that God creates the sight of Christ's glory. This means that when God enables us to see Christ in the gospel, in that very instant we are seeing him *as glorious*. We are not seeing him neutrally, equally ready to tilt toward being bored or being ravished. The gift of sight is the gift of *believing* sight.

There is no coercion in this sight. It is like awakening from a stupor in the foothills of the Alps. There is no coercion to cause us to be amazed at the peaks surrounding us. They are what they are, and they are self-authenticating in their glory. We do not ponder whether to find them dreary or dazzling. The awakening is the gift of seeing them for what they are, and thus the mountains are self-authenticating as magnificent. That is what I am saying about the glory of Christ in the gospel. To the blind, it is foolishness, but to those who see, it is what it is and cannot be otherwise—it is glorious, beautiful, precious beyond words.

Seeing Christ Is Not an Illusion

I hope it is obvious, therefore, that when I say that saving faith includes the sight of spiritual reality, I am not talking about illusions. I am not talking about visions. I am not talking about any dreams or imaginations or trance-like fantasies. Paul roots the glory of Christ in the gospel (2 Cor. 4:4)—in history. The glory of Christ is not seen in a dream; it is seen in the gospel—in the true facts and meaning of the death and resurrection of Jesus Christ.

Or we can be more general and say that the glory of Christ is seen in all of God's word. When Jesus said (through "father Abraham" in heaven) in Luke 16:31, "If they do not hear Moses and the Prophets, neither will they be convinced if someone should rise from the dead," he implied that there is so much self-authenticating divine glory in the Scriptures that the failure to see it means you will not see it in a resurrection either. This is why I say that the spiritual reality that the eyes of faith see shines *throughout* God's inspired word, not just in one part of it. Thus, the faith-seen glory of all that God is for us in Christ is not a free-floating brightness of a vision or a dream; it is the beauty of Christ revealed in the gospel story and in all the word of God.

I conclude, therefore, that saving faith includes spiritual sight of reality, especially the self-authenticating glory of Christ. This has huge implications. I will argue in chapter 16 that the divine gift of spiritual sight, which perceives the glory of Christ, cannot but see and experience him as a treasure. For if a believer and an unbeliever look at the same gospel story, with the same amount of explanation, but the unbeliever sees foolishness and the believer sees beauty and greatness and worth (glory!), how can this sight of the believer not be a treasuring, cherishing, admiring sight?

10

The Substance of Things Hoped For

(Clarification 7)

Clarification 7

Saving faith is "the substance of things hoped for." That is, faith is the present experience of the future realities that God has promised, especially the glory and worth of Christ. Future realities stream back into the present, as it were, and are tasted by faith.

The key passage behind this point is Hebrews 11:1 and its wider context in that book: "Now faith is the assurance [or *substance*] of things hoped for, the conviction of things not seen." This is the closest we get to an explicit definition of faith in the New Testament. The word translated *assurance* (ὑπόστασις, *hupostasis*) has also been translated *substance* ("Now faith is the *substance* of things hoped for," KJV). What is the difference in meaning between *assurance* and *substance*, and which is closer to the author's intention?

Substance or Assurance?

The word *hupostasis* is used two other times in the book of Hebrews. In Hebrews 1:3, we read, "[Christ] is the radiance of the glory of God and the exact imprint of his *nature* [ὑποστάσεως, *hupostaseōs*]." In Hebrews 3:14, it says, "We have come to share in Christ, if indeed we hold our original *confidence* [ὑποστάσεως, *hupostaseōs*] firm to the end." To be precise, there is no word for *our* in the Greek of Hebrews 3:14. More literally it says, "We have come to share in Christ, if indeed the beginning of the *hupostaseōs* we hold firm to the end." In the other two New Testament occurrences of *hupostasis* outside of Hebrews, they appear to mean *confidence* (2 Cor. 9:4; 11:17).

On the one hand, the writer of Hebrews uses the word to refer to God's nature, essence, substance, or reality as it comes to expression in the incarnate Christ (1:3). On the other hand, he uses the word to refer to the inner state of confidence or firmness of conviction (3:14). There are reasons why I doubt that this writer wants us to separate these two meanings.

Why Use a Loaded Word?

First, in Hebrews 11:1, if he wanted to express only *assurance*, he had at his disposal, just from the vocabulary he used in this letter, other words to capture that idea. He could have used *plērophoria* (πληροφορία, 6:11; 10:22) or *parrēsia* (παρρησία, 3:6; 4:16; 10:19, 35), both of which carry the sense of assurance or confidence. But he chose this loaded word, *hupostasis*.

I say the word is "loaded" because, in the very first paragraph of his letter, he loaded it with as much weight as any word can carry: Christ is the exact imprint of God's *hupostaseōs*! It is difficult for me to believe that, as the writer chose his words for how to define faith in the lead sentence of a chapter entirely designed to illustrate faith, he would not realize that he had signaled a profound meaning for *hupostasis* in his very first paragraph (1:3). No. I think he intended us to have that meaning (nature, substance, essence, reality) in mind as we read Hebrews 11:1.

Hupostasis Points to the Foundation of Assurance

Second, in using the word *hupostasis* to define faith in Hebrews 11:1 ("the *substance* of things hoped for"), the writer forces us to face the *basis* of assurance. Even if the word is used for *assurance* at times, it does not mean *merely* assurance. It connotes as well the *reality* or the *substance* under the assurance. It connotes a *warranted* assurance, an assurance resting on, or participating in, something real, something substantial.

In other words, in Hebrews 11:1, *hupostasis* describes faith as the present experience of the *substance* of a future reality ("things hoped for"). The future reality becomes in some measure *substantially present*. This is what faith is. It is the experience of that substance. It *sees*, or one could say *tastes*, the present reality of the thing hoped for. The spiritual, unseen reality becomes, in faith, real and substantial. The coming glory and worth of Christ are known as real in faith now.

"Joy Set before Him"

Third, the way Hebrews illustrates faith as "the substance of things hoped for" shows us how this substance is known in faith and how it works powerfully in our lives as something real. To see this, consider first the power that "things hoped for" had in the last hours of Jesus's life:

> Since we are surrounded by so great a cloud of witnesses, let us also lay aside every weight, and sin which clings so closely, and

let us run with endurance the race that is set before us, looking to Jesus, the founder and perfecter of our faith, who *for the joy that was set before him endured the cross*, despising the shame, and is seated at the right hand of the throne of God. (Heb. 12:1–2)

As we endure our trials, we are to take Jesus as our example (Heb. 12:3–4). We are to "[look] to Jesus." Specifically, we are to take notice of how he "endured the cross," namely, "for the joy that was set before him"—the joy of resurrection, and sitting at God's right hand (Heb. 1:3), surrounded by "innumerable angels in festal gathering" (Heb. 12:22) and a cloud of witnesses, the righteous redeemed (Heb. 12:1, 23). In other words, Jesus was able to endure the cross because of how real in his own soul were the "things hoped for"—the joy set before him.

Jesus is given as an example for us to follow in how to endure suffering *by faith*. The reality, the substance, of things hoped for was powerfully effective in the present in Jesus's life, enabling him to love people to the uttermost. This, I am suggesting, is the way Hebrews 11:1 is to be understood. To put it another way, "the joy that was set before him" was not merely "before him" at a great distance; it was "before him" as an experienced reality. By faith, as it says in Hebrews 11:27, he could see the unseen. The "substance" of what was hoped for—the essential spiritual reality, the well-founded joy before him—became by faith a present, sustaining power in Jesus's last hours.

"You Knew That You . . . Had a Better Possession"

This understanding of faith in Hebrews 12:2 and 11:1 is confirmed by other texts in Hebrews. For example, when the Christian believers in Hebrews 10:32–34 followed the example of Jesus by enduring suffering with joy, how did they do it? They did it like this: "You had compassion on those in prison, and you joyfully accepted the plundering of your property, *since you knew that you yourselves had a better possession and an abiding one*" (v. 34).

This is the same pattern of motivation that we saw in Jesus's final hours. Jesus looked to "the joy set before him." The Christians looked to the "better possession and . . . abiding one." Jesus loved his own at the cost of his life. They loved the prisoners at the cost of their possessions. As they looked to the reward of God's presence in the resurrection, they "knew" it was theirs. "You *knew* that you yourselves had a better possession."

This "knowing" is the "seeing the unseen" that Jesus experienced. The joy set before them—the better and abiding possession—became in the hearts of the believers the "substance of the things hoped for." The joy of the future glory was experienced in the present. "You *joyfully* accepted the plundering of your property." This utterly counterintuitive joy in the midst of loss was the miraculous experience of the substance of the future joy streaming back into the present. Thus, we may say, as is said so many times in Hebrews 11, "by faith" the believers loved their brothers, and endured affliction. The better and abiding possession that was hoped for became a substantial reality in the present. It was "seen" and "known" with stunning power. This is the ongoing reality of saving faith.

"He Was Looking to the Reward"

Consider one more example of this understanding of faith and its love-producing power as the substance of things hoped for:

> *By faith* Moses, when he was grown up, refused to be called the son of Pharaoh's daughter, choosing rather to be mistreated

with the people of God than to enjoy the fleeting pleasures of sin. He considered the reproach of Christ greater wealth than the treasures of Egypt, for he was looking to the reward. (Heb. 11:24–26)

Moses did three things "by faith." (1) By faith he "refused to be called the son of Pharaoh's daughter." (2) By faith he chose to be "mistreated with the people of God" instead of having Egypt's "fleeting pleasures of sin." (3) By faith he "considered the reproach of Christ" worth more "than the treasures of Egypt."

These sacrifices correspond to Jesus's enduring the cross in Hebrews 12:2 and the Christians' enduring the loss of their possessions in Hebrews 10:34. Then comes the explanation for how Moses did this "by faith": "for he was looking to the reward" (11:26). This corresponds to Jesus's looking to the "joy set before him," and the Christians' "knowing" that they had a better possession and an abiding one.

When it says Moses "[looked] to the reward," it does not mean he looked and saw nothing of substance. The very next verse says, "By faith he left Egypt . . . *as seeing him who is invisible*" (11:27). He did not just look. He saw. And what he saw was the Messiah (τοῦ Χριστοῦ, *tou Christou*, v. 26). And this hoped-for Messiah was the reward. What he saw was so real in the promises of God that we may say Moses's faith became the substance of things hoped for.

So my seventh clarification is that saving faith is the substance of things hoped for. It is the present experience of the future realities that God has promised, especially the glory and worth of Christ. In saving faith, future realities become real in the sense that they are spiritually "tasted" (1 Pet. 2:3). They are "seen" by the eyes of the heart (Eph. 1:18).

We will return to Hebrews 11:1 and this aspect of the nature of faith in chapter 17. Here the focus has simply been on faith as the realization in the present of hoped-for reality. There the focus will be on the affectional nature of that realization. No doubt, a discerning reader has noticed that the power of joy was at work in the case of Jesus, the early Christians, and Moses. But that has not been the main point here. It will be in chapter 17, because there the question will be, How can the substance of hoped-for joy not itself be joy?

11

The Root of All God-Pleasing Works

(Clarification 8)

Clarification 8

Saving faith is not a work—not an act of the will or the body—
that calls attention to itself as the basis of our right standing
with God. This is true even though faith is a good gift of God.
Rather, saving faith (including justifying faith) is the means God
uses to enable us to will and to do good works.[1]

---

1 I don't equate salvation and justification, even though some texts may use the idea of
"being saved" when the focus is mainly on "being justified" (e.g., Eph. 2:8–9). The reason
is that the reality of salvation is much more comprehensive than the reality of justification.
Justification refers to the act of God at a point in time when an individual is counted
righteous in union with Christ by the instrument of faith alone. *Salvation* refers to the
entire work of God from eternity to eternity by which he does all that is needed to bring
sinners into eternal, joyful perfection and fellowship with himself. Thus Paul speaks of a
believer's salvation as belonging to his past (Eph. 2:8, "you have been saved") and present
(1 Cor. 1:18, "who are being saved") and future (Rom. 13:11, "salvation is nearer to us
now than when we first believed"). I do not see any significant difference between the
faith that connects us with Christ for justification and the faith that I must persevere in
for final salvation.

The Basis of God's Being for Us Is Outside Us

Faith does not look to itself as the ground or the basis for why God is 100 percent for us as believers in Christ.[2] The basis of why God is 100 percent for us is not *in* us—not in our faith, not in our good disposition, not in our virtue, not in our outward acts of love. The basis of God's being 100 percent for us is *outside* of us, not in us. It is in the death and righteousness of Christ. "Christ died for the *ungodly*" (Rom. 5:6). "While we were still *sinners*, Christ died for us" (Rom. 5:8). "[God] justifies the *ungodly*" (Rom. 4:5). "While we were *enemies* we were reconciled to God by the death of his Son" (Rom. 5:10). "By the one man's obedience the many will be appointed righteous" (Rom. 5:19, my translation). "Not having a righteousness of my own that comes from the law, but . . . the righteousness from God that depends on faith" (Phil. 3:9).

All God-Commanded Duty Comes from Saving Faith

This saving faith is a kind of reality in the soul that moves the believer to love people.[3] That is the meaning of Galatians 5:6: "In Christ Jesus neither circumcision nor uncircumcision counts for anything, but only *faith working through love*." In other words, faith

2 Speaking of God as 100 percent for us is my way of referring to being *justified* by God: "If God is *for* us, who can be against us? . . . It is God who justifies" (Rom. 8:31, 33). I use this phrase, "100 percent for us," to underline the astonishing and wonderful reality that from the moment of justification, and then forever, there is no hint of disinclination in God to work for our everlasting joy. After our union with Christ and the removal of God's wrath and the declaration of our righteous standing, there is no moment when God is not for us, and there is no fading by degrees of his being for us—hence, "100 percent for us." Our postconversion sins may grieve the Spirit (Eph. 4:30), but they do not diminish, even by .001 percent, God's commitment to be for us forever.

3 For my detailed exegetical argument for this understanding of Gal. 5:6, see appendix 3, "Thoughts on Galatians 5:6 and the Relationship between Faith and Love," in John Piper, *The Future of Justification: A Response to N. T. Wright* (Wheaton, IL: Crossway, 2007), 203–6.

alone is the instrument of justification,[4] but this justifying faith is the kind of reality that moves the believer to love people. I say "love *people*" because it is clear from the context of Galatians 5:6 that this is what love refers to. The same phrase ("through love") occurs in the following context with this meaning: "*Through love* serve one another" (Gal. 5:13).

In the next verse, Galatians 5:14, Paul supports this kind of faith-produced love by saying, "For the whole law is fulfilled in one word: 'You shall love your neighbor as yourself.'" He says the same thing in Romans 13:8: "The one who loves another has fulfilled the law." With these words, Paul speaks comprehensively about all human duty before God. When we love people as we ought, all God-commanded duty for believers is fulfilled. Therefore, saving faith is the spring of every God-pleasing act of the will that is not part of saving faith. Or to put it negatively: "Whatever does not proceed from faith is sin" (Rom. 14:23).

Work of Faith

Paul underlines repeatedly this crucial and powerful relationship between faith and the good works of love. Paul would happily say with James, "I will show you my faith *by my works*" (James 2:18). For the works of love are the fruit of faith, and thus the aim of

---

4 "We hold that one is justified by faith apart from works of the law" (Rom. 3:28). "If it is the adherents of the law who are to be the heirs, faith is null and the promise is void" (Rom. 4:14). "We have been justified by faith" (Rom. 5:1). "What shall we say, then? That Gentiles who did not pursue righteousness have attained it, that is, a righteousness that is by faith" (Rom. 9:30). "We know that a person is not justified by works of the law but through faith in Jesus Christ . . . because by works of the law no one will be justified" (Gal. 2:16). "It is evident that no one is justified before God by the law, for 'The righteous shall live by faith'" (Gal. 3:11). "I testify again to every man who accepts circumcision that he is obligated to keep the whole law. You are severed from Christ, you who would be justified by the law; you have fallen away from grace" (Gal. 5:3–4).

Paul's ministry. "The aim of our charge is *love that issues from . . . sincere faith*" (ἐκ . . . πίστεως ἀνυποκρίτου, *ek . . . pisteōs anupokritou*, 1 Tim. 1:5).

Paul calls the God-pleasing works of believers "works of *faith*," meaning that their faith is the kind of reality that moves them to do good works. For example, in his prayers for the Thessalonians, he remembers their "work of faith" (ἔργου τῆς πίστεως, *ergou tēs pisteōs*, 1 Thess. 1:3). And he prays "that our God may . . . fulfill every resolve for good and every *work of faith* [ἔργον πίστεως, *ergon pisteōs*] by his power" (2 Thess. 1:11). A Christian's good works are "works of faith," meaning they are the fruit of the transforming effects of faith.

Saved by Faith for Love

In Paul's mind, saving faith is the gracious work of God in us (Acts 13:48; 2 Cor. 4:6; Phil. 1:29) that is designed by God for two distinct and glorious effects. First, it is the instrument of justification. That is, God instantaneously and simultaneously unites us to Christ and counts us righteous before him for Christ's sake when our faith comes into being (see chapter 5, note 16). Second, this saving faith is the kind of reality that moves us to love others—that is, to live in a way that does good works and fulfills the law.

Both of these designs of saving faith are seen in Ephesians 2:8–10:

By grace you have been saved through faith. And this is not your own doing; it is the gift of God, not a result of works, so that no one may boast. For we are his workmanship, created in Christ Jesus for good works, which God prepared beforehand, that we should walk in them.

Salvation by grace through faith is called God's "workmanship" (ποίημα, *poiēma*). It is God's creation. When God works by grace to bring a believer into being, Paul describes this as being "created in Christ Jesus." Believers are new creatures (2 Cor. 5:17). This "workmanship" of new "creation"—this bringing of faith into being—has a double design. The faith saves instantaneously ("have been saved," ἐστε σεσῳσμένοι, *este sesōsmenoi*, v. 8), and it brings about good works ("created . . . for good works," v. 10). Saving faith is the kind of reality that saves the soul from the wrath of God (Eph. 2:3) and moves the believer to love others.

Is Love a Fruit of Faith or a Fruit of the Spirit?

When I argue that every God-pleasing act of the will (summed up in love) is the fruit of saving faith, I am not denying that it is also the fruit of the Spirit. Clearly, "the fruit of the Spirit is love" (Gal. 5:22). So how do our faith and God's Spirit connect with each other in bearing the fruit of love? Paul clarifies the connection between faith and the Spirit in Galatians 3:5: "Does he who supplies the Spirit to you and works miracles among you do so by works of the law, or by hearing with faith . . . ?" The answer he expects is "hearing with faith."

In other words, the Spirit is given to us when we first hear the word of God with faith (Gal. 3:2, 5, 14). And the Spirit goes on being powerfully active in believers as we go on hearing God's word with faith. So the fruit of the Spirit is also the fruit of faith. The Spirit does his work in and through faith. Faith does its work by the Spirit.

So my eighth clarification of saving faith is meant mainly to draw attention to the fact that faith not only justifies instantaneously (in our union with Christ) but also moves believers to love people.[5] It is that kind of reality. It has that kind of nature. It is an amazing force. It becomes powerfully effective through love (δι' ἀγάπης ἐνεργουμένη, *di' agapēs energoumenē*, Gal. 5:6). This love for people is *not* love for Christ. This love for our neighbor is the *fruit* of faith, not *part* of faith. Saving faith is so pervasively effective in producing this love that we may say that every God-pleasing act of the will that is not part of saving faith is the fruit of saving faith.[6]

When we turn in parts 3 and 4 to the biblical foundations of the affectional nature of saving faith, part of our question will be whether the affectional dimension (such as treasuring Christ, loving Christ, being satisfied with all that God is for us in Christ) is the key to why saving faith has this remarkable transforming power.

---

5 The reason I think *love* in Gal. 5:6 refers to love for people or neighbor and does not include love for God or Christ is that the phrase *through love* (δι' ἀγάπης) in 5:6 occurs again in 5:13: "You were called to freedom, brothers. Only do not use your freedom as an opportunity for the flesh, but through love [διὰ τῆς ἀγάπης] serve one another." Thus the love in Paul's mind in this context is love for "one another."

6 For a more detailed defense of this understanding of Gal. 5:6, see John Piper, *The Future of Justification* (Wheaton, IL: Crossway, 2007), 203–6.

12

A Supernatural Creation of God

(Clarification 9)

Clarification 9

As a supernatural creation by God, saving faith is not a natural reality. It cannot be produced by a human being apart from God's supernatural intervention. Therefore, it is different from any faith that demons or man can have apart from a supernatural new birth.

The point here is not merely that faith is a gift of God. To be sure, it is a gift of God. The apostle John writes, "Everyone who *believes* that Jesus is the Christ *has been born* of God" (1 John 5:1). John Stott observes, "The combination of present tense (*ho pisteuōn, believes*) and perfect ['has been born'] is important. It shows clearly that believing is the consequence, not the cause, of the new birth."[1]

---

1   John R. W. Stott, *The Letter of John: An Introduction and Commentary*, vol. 19, Tyndale New Testament Commentaries (Downers Grove, IL: InterVarsity Press, 1988), 172.

Being born again supernaturally is no more in our control than being born naturally was in our control. It is no more in our control than the wind. Which is why Jesus said, "The wind blows where it wishes, and you hear its sound, but you do not know where it comes from or where it goes. So it is with everyone who is born of the Spirit" (John 3:8). Saving faith is the defining reality of those who are born again. The new thing God brings into being in the new birth is the new reality of saving faith.

Being a New Creation Makes Faith a New Kind of Faith

So, yes, it is true that faith is a gift of God. But the fact that faith is a gift does not get to the main point I want to make here. Often when we say that faith is a gift, we are simply trying to make clear that we cannot take credit for it and that God is sovereign, and our ability to believe is owing decisively to him in the moment of our conversion. I agree with all of that. But it does not yet draw out the implication I am focusing on—namely, that as a work of God, faith is therefore supernaturally peculiar in its nature. It's not like ordinary, natural belief, or natural faith—*natural* in the sense Paul uses the word in 1 Corinthians 2:14 ("natural person"): what a person is, and can do, as a mere human, apart from the supernatural work of the Spirit.

One might say that the ability to jog at the age of seventy is owing to the fact that good knee joints are a gift of God. That would be true. In the same way, one might say that faith is a gift. It's like good joints. But good joints are natural. The fact that they are ultimately a gift of God does not make them supernatural—not in the way I am using the word. That's the way some people think about faith—namely, God *gives* it, but it is, for all that, *natural* like any other wise decision or act of trust.

But that is not what I am saying. I am arguing that *the way* God gives or creates or brings about saving faith imparts to his new creature a supernatural newness, including a kind of faith, that is *not* natural. It bears the marks of God's handiwork. Just as the new birth is supernatural, so, in the same way, what it brings about is supernatural. Therefore, saving faith is what it is, in significant measure, because it is the workmanship of a supernatural Creator, bringing into being something that cannot come into being from resources present in fallen human nature.

Faith Is the New Experience of Christ's Glory in the New Creation

We can see the supernatural character of saving faith by briefly revisiting 2 Corinthians 4:4–6, which was important above under clarification 6 (chapter 9). Second Corinthians 4:6 is describing the new birth in other terms. The situation is that all of us at one time, in our unbelief, were blind to the glory of God in the gospel. "The god of this world has blinded the minds of the unbelievers, to keep them from seeing the light of the gospel of the glory of Christ, who is the image of God" (2 Cor. 4:4). A miracle of divine intervention was needed to remove the blindness and give a new sight of divine glory. That happened in verse 6. It is the new birth described as new creation and new sight.

"God, who said, 'Let light shine out of darkness,' has shone in our hearts to give the light of the knowledge of the glory of God in the face of Jesus Christ" (2 Cor. 4:6). This is the creation of saving faith. By virtue of this supernatural light and accompanying blindness removal, saving faith springs to life with the supernatural sight of "the glory of God in the face of Jesus Christ." I argued under clarification 6 that this sight is part of what saving faith is.

Here I am simply stating the obvious implication: as a supernatural creation by God, saving faith is not a natural reality. There is an experience of divine glory of which no natural person is capable. Therefore, saving faith is supernaturally different from any faith that demons or man can have apart from a supernatural new birth.

God Brings Faith into Being by Freeing
from Bondage to Boasting

Consider another mark of the supernatural nature of saving faith. In Romans 3:26, Paul concludes that God is "just and the justifier of the one who has faith in Jesus." Then to draw out an aspect of this faith, he asks, "Then what becomes of our boasting? It is excluded. By what kind of law? By a law of works? No, but by the law of faith. For we hold that one is justified by faith apart from works of the law" (Rom. 3:27–28). In other words, saving faith is the kind of reality that takes boasting out of the human heart. This is a very powerful transformation, since pride is the essence of fallen human nature. Faith has in it pride-killing power.

Not surprisingly, then, Jesus describes the fallen heart's love for human glory as an obstacle to saving faith. No, not just an obstacle, but an *insuperable* obstacle—apart from new birth. He says:

I have come in my Father's name, and you do not receive me. If another comes in his own name, you will receive him. How can you believe, when you receive glory from one another and do not seek the glory that comes from the only God? (John 5:43–44)

This rhetorical question is in reality a statement. "How can you believe . . ." means "You can't believe . . ." Not while your heart is under the sway of the love of human praise. If someone comes to you in "his own name," you will receive him. But if I come to you *not* in my own name, you reject me. Why? Because coming in my own name would confirm your own love affair with self-exaltation. I would be like you, seeking my own glory in my own name. I would fit with your pride. Being one like you, I would bless your bondage to boasting. You would welcome me.

But instead, I come in my Father's name, and "you do not receive me" (5:43). No. Not just *do* not, but *cannot.* "How *can* you believe, when you receive glory from one another?" (see Rom. 8:7–8; 1 Cor. 2:14). Saving faith, as in John 1:12, is equated with "receiving" Jesus. And it can't be done by those who are in bondage to boasting in man.

This implies that when God creates saving faith through the new birth (John 3:8; 1 John 5:1), he creates something beyond the natural. It is beyond the natural to eliminate boasting. It is beyond the natural to experience a preference for the glory of God over the glory of man. But when saving faith comes into being, that is what happens.

So my ninth clarification of saving faith is that, as a supernatural creation by God, saving faith is not a natural reality. It is supernaturally different from any faith that demons or man can have apart from a supernatural new birth.

Multifaceted, Nonexhaustive

The overarching purpose of part 2 has been to give a general description of saving faith in the New Testament. I have tried to do this with nine clarifications. They are not an exhaustive description of faith. In fact, I would say that saving faith is such multifaceted reality—such a living, experienced reality in the human soul—that it is impossible to be exhaustive.[2]

---

2 Herman Bavinck said, "The descriptions that have been given of faith since the Reformation are so numerous and divergent as to make a person almost despair of the possibility of

The reason for clarifying the *general* meaning of saving faith in the New Testament is so that we will not be using the term *saving faith* in the rest of this book without any content. I want us to have a general sense of what saving faith is, so that we can have a starting place from which now to ask, Does the New Testament teach that saving faith includes affectional elements? Does the New Testament show that saving faith, in its very nature, has affectional dimensions like treasuring Christ, or loving Christ, or enjoying Christ, or being satisfied in Christ?

As it turns out, providing this broader, more general sense of what saving faith is does more than give us a nonexhaustive description with which to proceed. It also points to the very thing we will find in parts 3 and 4. More than once, our effort to come to terms with the general meaning of saving faith has made its affectional nature seem inevitable. So we turn now to focus specifically on texts that teach that this seemingly inevitable reality is actually there.

---

correctly and clearly defining the nature of faith." Herman Bavinck, John Bolt, and John Vriend, *Reformed Dogmatics: Holy Spirit, Church, and New Creation*, vol. 4 (Grand Rapids, MI: Baker Academic, 2008), 121. The reason for this is not only that human interpreters are finite and fallible, but also, and more to my point, that, as Herman Witsius said, "[Saving faith] is a certain complex thing, consisting of various acts, which, without confusion pervade, and by a sweet and happy conjunction, mutually promote and assist one another." Herman Witsius, *The Economy of the Covenants between God and Man: Comprehending a Complete Body of Divinity*, trans. William Crookshank, vol. 1 (London: T. Tegg & Son, 1837), 337. In other words, faith is such a living reality, responding to and reflecting rationally and affectionally such immeasurable glories of Christ, that to think of exhaustively defining or describing it is folly.

PART 3

RECEIVING CHRIST AS OUR SUPREME TREASURE

One of the most important clarifications we made in part 2 about the nature of saving faith was that it is a *receiving* (chapter 8). Faith justifies not because it is the right thing to do, but because it *receives* Christ. The experience of faith is always a kind of *receiving*. The question we turn to now is this: Is saving faith a receiving of Christ *as the soul's supreme treasure?*

Receiving Christ as a Treasure in All His Glories

I don't ask this to exclude from faith the receiving of Christ as *Savior* or as *Lord*, or to exclude the receiving of any other aspect of his greatness. I am simply focusing on his reality as treasure—as when Jesus says, "The kingdom of heaven is like *treasure* hidden in a field" (Matt. 13:44), or when Paul writes, "We have this *treasure* in jars of clay" (2 Cor. 4:7).

In fact, as I mentioned in the introduction, when I focus on Jesus as our treasure, I include *all* that he is: treasured Savior, treasured Lord, treasured wisdom, treasured righteousness, treasured friend, and so on. If it turns out (as I will argue now in part 3) that saving faith is, in fact, a receiving of Christ *as the soul's supreme treasure,* then the question will become, How does this receiving of Christ *as a treasure* determine or shape the nature of faith (part 4)?

Why Distinguish Treasuring and Receiving as a Treasure?

To distinguish between treasuring and receiving as a treasure may seem to you like splitting hairs. If saving faith really does receive Christ as a treasure (part 3), why would I need to describe how this reality shapes the nature of faith (part 4)? If faith receives Christ as a *treasure,* doesn't that mean faith *treasures* Christ? How are they even different? Frankly, as I normally use this language, receiving Christ as a treasure and treasuring Christ are not different. Ordinarily, I use these terms interchangeably.

But there are two reasons why I am distinguishing them and devoting a separate part of this book to each. First, given how flexible and ambiguous words can be, and given how convoluted mental and emotional processes can be, someone is likely to say that they do, in fact, receive Christ as their supreme treasure but do not treasure him supremely. I'm not talking here about the ordinary fight of faith that all true believers experience—the daily battle to fix our eyes on Christ as supreme and fan the flames of saving faith. We will deal with that in chapter 26. I'm talking about people who "acknowledge" Christ as a supreme treasure but have no experience of treasuring Christ as supreme, nor do they think this necessary as part of saving faith. And they are quite content to believe that such affectional experiences are part of a super spirituality, which they do not aspire to. But they see themselves as Christians.

So I can imagine such people insisting that I split these hairs. Yes, they say, there are texts that show that saving faith receives Christ as a treasure. But, they also say, that does not prove that this "receiving of Christ as a treasure" is in fact an affectional experience of the heart. Saving may be a "receiving" of a treasure without treasuring the treasure—as a person might receive an inheritance of an estate which they have no interest in owning. They are eager to cash it in for what they really want. So to deal as meticulously and precisely as I can with the biblical texts, I will first make the case that saving faith receives Christ as a supreme treasure (part 3), and then I will seek to make the added case from Scripture that this receiving of Christ as a treasure is in fact a treasuring of Christ—an affectional dimension of saving faith (part 4).

Testing John Owen's Insight

The second reason for distinguishing the concerns of parts 3 and 4 is that it accords with the fact that the affectional nature of saving faith really is determined by the nature of the Christ we receive. Focusing on the receiving of that Christ in part 3 and the consequent nature of the receiving in part 4 underlines the importance of this connection between the infinite worth of Christ and the affectional nature of faith.

When the Holy Spirit creates saving faith in the new birth, he sets Christ before us and removes our blindness. But the nature of the faith that comes into being at that moment is determined both by the gift of new eyes and by the beauty and worth of what is seen. The great Puritan theologian John Owen writes:

Faith brings into the soul an experience of [the] power and efficacy [of the unseen things that are believed], whereby [the soul] is cast into the mold of them, or made conformable unto them.[1]

So our task in part 3 is to make the case that saving faith is, in part, a receiving of Christ as our supreme treasure. I admit that it will be difficult not to speak of this as treasuring Christ. But I am going to make the effort. Then, in part 4, we will put Owen to the test: Does the nature of Christ as a received treasure "cast the believer's soul into the [affectional!] mold" of treasuring Christ? Does receiving Christ as our supreme treasure "make the soul [affectionally!] conformable" to Christ's value? That is, does saving faith have the affectional dimension of heartfelt treasuring?

---

1 John Owen, *An Exposition of the Epistle to the Hebrews*, vol. 24, *The Works of John Owen*, ed. William H. Goold (Edinburgh: Johnstone & Hunter, 1854), 12.

13

Saving Faith Receives
Christ, but Not in Vain

IN THIS CHAPTER, we briefly refocus on saving faith as receiving Christ, but we also remind ourselves that not all receiving is saving. Keep in mind that when I refer to receiving Christ, I don't limit this receiving to the first act of saving faith. I argued in chapter 8 that saving faith is both the *first* act of receiving Christ (John 1:12; Col. 2:6), and the *ongoing* spirit of welcoming him and depending on him hour by hour (Gal. 2:20; Eph. 3:17). Saving faith is lifelong, persevering faith, not just the act by which we first become Christians. We will see that not to persevere is never to have had saving faith.

Believing Christ Is Receiving Christ

As we saw in chapter 8, Jesus, John, and Paul connect saving faith (believing) with receiving Christ.

Jesus:

> I have come in my Father's name, and you do not *receive* me. If another comes in his own name, you will *receive* him. How

can you *believe*, when you receive glory from one another and do not seek the glory that comes from the only God? (John 5:43–44)

John:

[Jesus] came to his own, and his own people did not receive him. But to all who did *receive* him, who *believed* in his name, he gave the right to become children of God, who were born, not of blood nor of the will of the flesh nor of the will of man, but of God. (John 1:11–13)

Paul:

As you *received* Christ Jesus the Lord, so walk in him, rooted and built up in him and established in the *faith*, just as you were taught, abounding in thanksgiving. (Col. 2:6–7)

Faith that "receives" Christ is *saving* faith because receiving Christ means to *have* Christ. And "whoever has the Son has life" (1 John 5:12). Christ does not provide salvation as a distant giver. He provides salvation by being *received* and by being in union with us, which includes dwelling in us. This is one reason why Paul emphasizes the indwelling presence of Christ.

For example, Christ dwells "in [our] hearts through faith" (Eph. 3:17). "Christ . . . lives in me. And the life I now live in the flesh I live by faith in the Son of God" (Gal. 2:20). "Anyone who does not have the Spirit of Christ does not belong to him. But if Christ is in you . . . the Spirit is life because of righteousness" (Rom. 8:9–10). "Christ [is] in you, the hope of glory" (Col. 1:27).

Therefore, saving faith *receives* Christ. There is no salvation where Christ is not received. Therefore, faith that does not receive Christ is not *saving* faith.

Lesson in My Inner-City Neighborhood

One of the reasons I am writing this book is that many people "receive Christ" as a sin forgiver because they treasure being guilt-free, not because they treasure Christ. Many people receive him as rescuer from hell because they treasure being pain-free, not because they treasure Christ. Many people receive him as a healer because they treasure being disease-free, not because they treasure Christ. They receive him as a protector because they treasure being safe, not because they treasure Christ. They receive him as a prosperity giver because they treasure being wealthy, not because they treasure Christ. Many claim to receive Christ and to be a Christian. But they do not receive him as a treasure.

I have lived in the same inner-city neighborhood for forty years. It is beset with every kind of breakdown and dysfunction—mental illness, family disintegration, drunkenness, drugs, unemployment, poverty, homelessness, and every level of crime, from loitering to homicide. I have spoken to hundreds of people in this neighborhood about Christ. And I think I could count on one hand the number of people who have denied Christ. They have all "received him." Chronically drunk people have received him. Drug dealers have received him. Prostitutes have received him. This kind of "receiving" of Christ is not a joy that I celebrate; it is a heartache that I bemoan.

Not Even His Brothers Believed

Jesus and his apostles were very aware of "faith" that is not saving faith—"receiving" that is not saving receiving. For example, John said, "Many believed in his name when they saw the signs that he was doing. But Jesus on his part did not entrust himself to them, because he knew all people. . . . He himself knew what was in man" (John 2:23–25). In other words, they "received" him as a miracle worker, but they did not have saving faith. Jesus's own brothers were in this category. "His brothers said to him, 'Leave here and go to Judea, that your disciples also may see the works you are doing.' . . . For not even his brothers believed in him" (John 7:2–3, 5).

Not only did some people "receive" Jesus as a miracle worker without being saved; some people (like Judas) even performed miracles themselves in Jesus's name, yet did not have saving faith:

> On that day many will say to me, "Lord, Lord, did we not prophesy in your name, and cast out demons in your name, and do many mighty works in your name?" And then will I declare to them, "I never knew you; depart from me, you workers of lawlessness." (Matt. 7:22–23)

Do Not Receive God's Grace in Vain

Paul taught the same: a person can do miracles by "faith" and not be saved. "If I have prophetic powers, and understand all mysteries and all knowledge, and if I *have all faith*, so as to remove mountains, but have not love, I am nothing" (1 Cor. 13:2). You can have mountain-moving faith and come to nothing.

James looked at the lives of some "believers" and said, "Faith apart from works is dead" (James 2:26). Dead faith is not saving faith. He went so far as to say, "Even the demons *believe*—and shudder!" (James 2:19). This is immensely important to remember, because the demons know more truth about Jesus than most humans do. For example, the unclean spirit in Mark 1:24 cried out to Jesus, "I know who you are—the Holy One of God." The demon spoke more truth than the Pharisees could see. The demons believe many true facts about Jesus. But none of them is saved.

As Paul assessed the results of his own preaching, he knew that some of the positive responses were not saving faith. He probably knew of Jesus's parable about the four soils, where Jesus speaks of some who, "when they hear the word, *receive* it with joy. But these have no root; they *believe* for a while, and in time of testing fall away" (Luke 8:13). Paul refers to this as believing "in vain":

> I would remind you, brothers, of the gospel I preached to you, which you received, in which you stand, and by which you are being saved, if you hold fast to the word I preached to you—*unless you believed in vain.* (1 Cor. 15:1–2)

He pleaded with people not to "receive" Christ in this way: "We appeal to you not to receive the grace of God in vain" (2 Cor. 6:1).

None of God's Elect Make Shipwreck

The apostle John knew that there were people in the church who were not truly saved. What are we to make of such "believers" when they finally forsake the faith? Both John and Paul taught that people who are truly born again and justified will, in fact, never forsake the faith; they will persevere in faith and be saved. They are eternally secure (John 10:27–29; Rom. 8:30).

So how is it that "believers" make shipwreck of their faith (1 Tim. 1:19) and are lost? John answers, "They went out from us, but they were not of us; for if they had been of us, they would have continued with us. But they went out, that it might become plain that they all are not of us" (1 John 2:19). They had a kind of "faith," but they were not truly "of us." They were not born of God. They did not have saving faith (1 John 5:1). They had *received* Christ, but it was not a saving receiving.

Receiving Christ as Treasure?

Now with this brief refocus on saving faith as receiving Christ, we turn to the more specific question of part 3—namely, Is this receiving of Christ a receiving of him *as a treasure*? Remember, we are saving until part 4 the even more specific question of whether such a receiving has affectional elements in it—whether *receiving* Christ as our supreme treasure is in fact a *treasuring* of Christ as our supreme treasure.

14

The Message of Jesus about His Supreme Value

WE TURN NOW from saving faith as receiving Christ to saving faith as receiving Christ *as our supreme treasure*. Keep in mind that I am not carving Christ into pieces to be received selectively, as if Christ-as-treasure were one among several options. As I said at the beginning of part 3 (and in the introduction), when I focus on Jesus as our treasure, I include *all* that he is: treasured Savior, treasured Lord, treasured wisdom, treasured righteousness, treasured friend, treasured hope, and every other way that he offers himself to us. Christ-as-treasure is not a slice of Christ. It is all of Christ viewed from the standpoint of his infinite value.

The King of the Kingdom Is the Treasure

Jesus said in Matthew 13:44, "The kingdom of heaven is like treasure hidden in a field, which a man found and covered up. Then in his joy he goes and sells all that he has and buys that field."

Clearly, the treasure in this parable is identified as the "kingdom"—the rule of Christ, both in future glory and in the King's present power and fellowship ("Behold, the kingdom of God is in the midst of you," Luke 17:21). "The kingdom of heaven is like a treasure hidden in a field." It does not say, "Jesus is the treasure." But as Jesus and the writers of the New Testament unfold the meaning of the kingdom, it becomes plain that the value of the kingdom derives from the value of Christ himself (the King!), and is inseparable from him.

When we "enter the kingdom" (Matt. 5:20), whose reign do we enter? When we "receive the kingdom" (Mark 10:15), what is the best gift that we are receiving in it? When Jesus proclaims the kingdom to be "at hand" (Mark 1:15), in whose person has it arrived? When the kingdom is said to "belong" to us (Mark 10:14), whose authority do we have? When Jesus says that the "kingdom of God is in the midst of you" (Luke 17:21), who is standing there among them?

The claim of Jesus to be the incarnate presence of the kingdom of God is perhaps most plain when he says, "If it is by the Spirit of God that I cast out demons, then the kingdom of God has come upon you" (Matt. 12:28). More than that, Jesus calls the kingdom "my kingdom" (John 18:36). Paul describes Christian conversion as being "transferred . . . to the kingdom of [God's] beloved Son" (Col. 1:13). And Peter calls our final salvation an "entrance into the eternal kingdom of our Lord and Savior Jesus Christ" (2 Pet. 1:11).

Therefore, even though in Matthew 13:44 Jesus says that "the *kingdom* of heaven is like treasure," it is fair to infer that he says this because *he himself* is supremely valuable. And the point of the parable is to underline the value of Christ by showing that he is more valuable than all of our possessions in this world. "In his joy he goes and sells *all that he has* and buys that field."

Selling All with Joy to Have Christ

Two realities give this sentence its force. First, he sells "all that he has" in order to have the treasure. The point is not that you can buy Christ. The point is that he is worth more than all you own— or could own. Second, he sells everything with "joy." In other words, the "sacrifices" we endure in taking Christ as our treasure are in fact no sacrifice—not ultimately (Luke 18:28–30). The losses are accepted joyfully. Because the gain is infinitely greater.

What then is the point of this one-verse parable (Matt. 13:44)? The primary point is that Christ, in his kingly greatness, is supremely valuable. The secondary point is that the way to have Christ as our treasure is to experience such a joy in his value that he is more to be desired than all our other possessions put together. With this secondary point, I have slipped over into the point to be made in part 4. Receive it as a foreshadowing of what's to come—namely, that receiving Jesus as our treasure really does imply joyfully treasuring him.

Renounce All You Have and Receive Me

The little parable of Matthew 13:44 is applied by Jesus in Luke 14:33. There Jesus says, "Any one of you who does not renounce all that he has cannot be my disciple." Here the *kingdom* language has fallen away. The message is riveted on Jesus himself. If we do not find him more valuable than all our possessions, we cannot be his disciples.

Jesus made the same point with the rich ruler who inquired about eternal life (Luke 18:18). "One thing you still lack. Sell all that you have and distribute to the poor, and you will have treasure in heaven; and *come, follow me*" (Luke 18:22). In other words, if you value me enough to open your money-grasping fist and let the money fall from your hand onto the poor and put your hand in mine as your new treasure, you will indeed have a treasure forever in heaven—me. But if you value your possessions more than me, you won't have me or eternal life.

Loving Jesus More than Family

Again, Jesus drives home the message in Matthew 10:37: "Whoever loves father or mother more than me is not worthy of me, and whoever loves son or daughter more than me is not worthy of me." The "love" in view here is not the kind of love God shows in dying for his unworthy enemies (Rom. 5:8). This is the kind of love that family members have for their most cherished relatives—a mother or father, a precious son or daughter. Jesus is saying, "You are not worthy of me unless I am more precious to you than your most precious family members."

To be "worthy" of Jesus doesn't mean to deserve his friendship. The word *worthy* (ἄξιος, *axios*) means fitting or suitable or appropriate, as when John the Baptist said, "Bear fruit *worthy* [ἄξιον, *axion*] of repentance" (Matt. 3:8, my translation). That is, bear fruit in keeping with repentance, as is fitting with repentance, appropriate to one who is repenting. So in Matthew 10:37, Jesus means, "It is not fitting that anyone should have me as their treasure who does not treasure me above all other relationships."

Through Salvation We Have Christ, the Treasure

I think it is fair to say that flowing through all four Gospels is a river that irrigates everything with its vitality. The river may be called "the unsearchable riches of Christ" (Eph. 3:8)—or more precisely, Christ, our immeasurably valuable treasure.

Christ is present in Scripture not mainly as a dispenser of gifts to be cherished, though he is that. He is present in all his gifts mainly as the one who is worthy of being treasured—the one who is himself supremely beautiful and valuable. He does all that he does, and reveals all that he reveals, so that "in everything he might be preeminent" (Col. 1:18). Ultimately, the aim of God's work in redemption is not that through Christ we might have salvation, but that through salvation we might have Christ—the all-satisfying treasure.

15

The Surpassing Worth of Knowing Christ Jesus

WHEN WE TURN TO Paul's letters to see how he develops this truth of Christ's supreme value, we discover that in his mind, saving faith includes receiving Christ as our supreme treasure. Paul did not create this connection between saving faith and the embrace of Christ as supremely valuable. It was already present in the teaching of Jesus, as we saw in the previous chapter. As we look at Philippians 3, it will sound familiar.

What Was Once the Treasure

In Philippians 3, Paul lists the reasons for his former "confidence in the flesh"—that is, his self-exalting religious achievements. This Jewish pedigree was all "gain" before Paul's conversion to Christ:

> . . . circumcised on the eighth day, of the people of Israel, of the tribe of Benjamin, a Hebrew of Hebrews; as to the law, a Pharisee;

as to zeal, a persecutor of the church; as to righteousness under the law, blameless. (Phil. 3:5–6)

But then Paul was radically converted. He met the risen Christ personally and saw him on the Damascus road in blinding glory. The result of this conversion was dramatic and leads to the connection between faith in Christ and receiving him as a treasure:

> Whatever gain I had, I counted as loss for the sake of Christ. Indeed, I count everything as loss because of the surpassing worth of knowing Christ Jesus my Lord. For his sake I have suffered the loss of all things and count them as rubbish, in order that I may gain Christ and be found in him, not having a righteousness of my own that comes from the law, but that which comes through faith in Christ, the righteousness from God that depends on faith. (Phil. 3:7–9)

On Account of the Surpassing Value of Knowing Christ

Let's do some careful observation of how Paul argues—that is, how he weaves his phrases and clauses together with connecting words. Three times he uses the Greek connecting word διά (*dia*) followed grammatically by the accusative case, which together mean "on account of" or "because of." For the sake of consistency, I will translate all three phrases as "on account of."

> Verse 7: "on account of Christ," I have regarded my Jewish pedigree as loss.

> Verse 8a: "on account of the surpassing value of knowing Christ," I go on regarding all things as loss.

Verse 8b: "on account of Christ," I suffered the loss of all things, and I go on counting them as rubbish.

The phrase "on account of Christ" by itself is ambiguous. It could mean "on account of his threatening," or "on account of his promise to pay," or "on account of his folly." Of course, none of those makes sense in this context. I'm just pointing out that the phrase *on account of* (διὰ/ *dia* + the accusative) does not by itself settle how the connections work.

But what is *not* ambiguous is the meaning of "on account of Christ" in verse 8a: "on account of *the surpassing value of knowing Christ.*" In this phrase, Paul tells us exactly why he regards not just his Jewish pedigree but "everything" as loss. It is because of how valuable it is to know Christ—because Christ is a supreme treasure.

Discovering that Christ is of more value than "all things" causes Paul to view all things compared to Christ as loss. Loss in what way? Paul answers, (1) loss as the treasure of his soul, and (2) loss as the ground of his confidence before God.

We see this double answer in verse 3: "We [Christians] are the [true] circumcision, who worship by the Spirit of God and glory in Christ Jesus and put no confidence in the flesh." In other words, (1) all things are loss as the ground of his confidence because he now "glories in Christ"—Christ is now the ground of his boasting, not his own achievements. And (2) all things are loss to Paul because "confidence in the flesh" is worthless, and that is what all things are apart from Christ.

Link between Saving Faith and Christ as a Treasure

Now comes the connecting word that leads us to the link between Christ as a treasure and saving faith. At the end of Philippians 3:8, we read, "*in order that* I may gain Christ . . ." This connecting phrase, *in order that* (ἵνα, *hina*), alerts us to the fact that what he's about to say is the aim or outcome of what he has just said. What has he just said? The value of Christ is so great to Paul that he counts everything as loss by comparison.

Actually, he doesn't just *count* everything as loss, but he has experienced in his soul such an inversion of what he treasures that there has been a real *experience* of loss (ἐζημιώθην, *ezēmiōthēn*, "*I have suffered the loss* of all things," v. 8). And when Paul experiences this loss, he doesn't do so with gritted teeth, knowing that Christians are supposed to choose Christ over other things. That's not the way he lives. He is a new creation (2 Cor. 5:17). His preferences are new (Rom. 8:5). There has been a real experience of gain and loss.

Gone from his heart is the preference for the world over Christ— for fame over Christ (Gal. 1:14), for money over Christ (Phil. 4:11, 17), for food and sex over Christ (1 Cor. 9:27), for power and comfort over Christ (2 Cor. 12:10). All these alternative treasures have been lost. Christ has become Paul's supreme treasure. That is what has gone before the words *in order that* (v. 8b). The words *in order that* mean that there's an aim or outcome of Paul's embracing Christ as his supreme treasure.

What is that aim or outcome? What comes after the words *in order that*? Paul puts it like this:

> . . . in order that I may gain Christ and be found in him, not having a righteousness of my own that comes from the law, but that which comes through faith in Christ, the righteousness from God that depends on faith. (Phil. 3:8b–9)

Actually, you can see that he states three aims: (1) that I may gain Christ, (2) that I may be found in Christ, and (3) that as a result of being "in Christ," I may have a righteousness that is not my own, not from law-keeping, but that is from God. So there is a threefold outcome of Paul's embracing Christ as his supreme treasure: Gain Christ. Be in Christ. Have righteousness from God.

The reason being "in Christ" and having "righteousness from God" are added to "gaining Christ" is not that "gaining Christ" is a defective outcome or a subordinate outcome. Rather, the reason is that without having a new divine righteousness in Christ, Paul could not have Christ. Without such a gift of righteousness, Paul would perish (Rom. 5:17). He must have Christ as a justifying Savior if he is to have him as a satisfying treasure. Christ as righteousness (1 Cor. 1:30) and Christ as a treasure are received together or not at all.

Two Ways into Union with Christ—That Are One

But what is most relevant for our question is this: Paul shows that gaining Christ and being in Christ come about not just in one way (signaled by the *in order that*), but in two ways—that turn out to be one. That is, he describes the pathway into union with Christ in two ways. Seeing the oneness of these two descriptions of how Paul gets into Christ is the key to seeing the relationship between saving faith and treasuring Christ.

First, the phrase *in order that* shows that Paul's being "found in Christ" and his having new divine righteousness come about because Christ is now Paul's supreme treasure. The flow of thought goes like this: "I have come to experience everything as loss and rubbish, with Christ as my supreme treasure, *in order that* I might be in Christ and have a new righteousness." So Paul's coming to experience Christ as his supreme treasure is *in order that* he might be in Christ. This was the experiential door to union with Christ. This was the miracle God performed to unite Paul to Christ.

But, second, verse 9 gives another description of how Paul gained Christ and how he was united to him and received the gift of righteousness. It came about "through faith." Paul says it twice. To paraphrase, he said, "I was found to be in Christ, with a righteousness from God *through faith in Christ*. I have a union with Christ and a divine righteousness *through faith in Christ*. It all depends on faith."

So Paul gives two answers to the question, How did you gain Christ? What was it that brought you into union with Christ? What was it that clothed you with righteousness not your own? Paul's first answer is this: I experienced a revolutionary conversion in which my heart underwent an utter reversal of what I treasure—Jesus became supreme. His second answer is this: it happened through faith in Jesus.

And my conclusion is that these are not different answers. They are not different experiences. Paul makes no effort to distinguish them or to sequence them. On the one hand, he says that union with Christ is the outcome (ἵνα, *hina*, v. 8) of receiving Christ as his treasure. On the other hand, he says that union with Christ is the outcome of faith (διὰ πίστεως, *dia pisteōs* . . . ἐπὶ τῇ πίστει, *epi tē pistei*, v. 9).

What we have seen in Philippians 3:7–9 makes it extremely unlikely that Paul could say, "I have faith in Christ, but do not have him as my supreme treasure." Nor is it probable that he could say, "I have Christ as my supreme treasure, but I do not have saving faith in him." Rather, these verses lead us to think that Paul would say, "I experienced union with Christ through the God-given experience of receiving Christ as my supreme treasure—that is, through saving faith."

16

We Have This Treasure
in Jars of Clay

NOW WE TURN TO another place in Paul where he connects Christ
as our treasure with saving faith. We focused already with some care
on 2 Corinthians 4:4–6 in chapter 9, where we discussed faith as
a way of seeing. Now, by adding verse 7 to our consideration, we
will draw out of this text the connection between receiving Christ
and receiving him *as a treasure*.

The god of this world has blinded the minds of the *unbelievers*,
to keep them from seeing the light of the gospel of the glory
of Christ, who is the image of God. For what we proclaim is
not ourselves, but Jesus Christ as Lord, with ourselves as your
servants for Jesus' sake. For God, who said, "Let light shine out
of darkness," has shone in our hearts to give the light of the
knowledge of the glory of God in the face of Jesus Christ. But
we have this *treasure* in jars of clay, to show that the surpassing
power belongs to God and not to us. (2 Cor. 4:4–7)

How a Believer Comes into Being

The mark of unbelievers is that they cannot *see* "the light of the gospel of the glory of Christ" (2 Cor. 4:4). This inability to see is called the blinding work of Satan: "The god of this world has *blinded* the minds of the unbelievers." What unbelievers are blind to is a kind of light that shines from the gospel. It is not physical light. Therefore, it is not seen with physical eyes. But it is light, and it is seen. It is an inner seeing. A spiritual seeing.

Paul speaks of the eyes of the heart in Ephesians 1:18. And in 2 Corinthians 3:18, he speaks of a kind of seeing that profoundly transforms: "We all, with unveiled face, *beholding the glory of the Lord, are being transformed* into the same image from one degree of glory to another. For this comes from the Lord who is the Spirit."

Paul knew that such seeing comes about through the preaching of the gospel and through conversion to Christ. He knew this because Jesus commissioned him to his ministry with the words, "I am sending you to *open their eyes*, so that they may turn from darkness to light and from the power of Satan to God" (Acts 26:17–18).

Similarly, Peter knew that becoming a Christian means spiritual sight and not physical sight. On the one hand, he said that the believers in the Dispersion to whom he is writing have never *seen* Christ (1 Pet. 1:8). On the other hand, he said we have been "called . . . out of darkness into his marvelous *light*" so that we may "proclaim [his] excellencies" (1 Pet. 2:9). We are to see the light of his glory and declare it.

So when Paul speaks of the creation of this spiritual *seeing* in 2 Corinthians 4:6, he is explaining how a *believer* comes into being.

In 4:4, the unbeliever cannot see "the light of the gospel of the glory of Christ." But in 4:6, God acts to take away the blindness. God speaks to the heart, as he spoke to the darkness on the first day of creation, "Let there be light." The effect of this sovereign act on the human heart is the creation of *light*—the "light of the knowledge of the glory of God in the face of Jesus Christ." It shines from the gospel into our hearts. We see with the eyes of the heart the glory of God in Christ. A believer is born.

From Boredom to Beholding Glory

Before the miracle of 2 Corinthians 4:6 happened to any of us, we heard the gospel story of Christ and *saw* it as boring or foolish or legendary or incomprehensible. We saw no compelling beauty or value in Christ. Then God "shone in our hearts," and we *saw* glory. This was not a decision. This was a sight. We went from blindness to seeing. When you go from blindness to seeing, there is no moment to decide whether you are seeing. It is not a choice. You cannot decide not to see in the act of seeing. And you cannot decide not to see *as glorious* what you see as glorious. That is the miracle God works in verse 6. Once we were seeing the gospel facts without seeing the beauty of Christ. Then God spoke, and we saw through the facts of the gospel the beauty of divine reality.

This seeing in 2 Corinthians 4:6 is conversion. It is the coming into being of a believer. Verse 4 describes "unbelievers," and verse 6 describes the creation of believers. One group is blind to the compelling glory of Christ. The other sees the glory of Christ as it really is—compelling. Or to put it another way, believers are granted to see and receive Christ as supremely glorious. This is the meaning of becoming a believer, or having saving faith.

After the Miracle, Treasure

Now, how does Paul describe this experience in the next verse (2 Cor. 4:7)? He says, "But we have this *treasure* in jars of clay, to show that the surpassing power belongs to God and not to us." The most natural meaning of this "treasure" in a jar of clay is what God has just created in us in 4:6: "the light of the knowledge of the glory of God in the face of Jesus Christ." The word *this* in verse 7 makes the connection specific. "We have *this* treasure." He is not speaking in broad, general terms. He is referring to a specific treasure, "this treasure," the one he just described.

We should not try to decide whether he means the *seeing* of the glory of Christ as the treasure or *the glory of Christ itself* as the treasure. Paul is not celebrating the presence of sight with no substance of what is seen. Nor is he celebrating the presence of the substance of glory to which we remain blind. The treasure is both the reality of Christ in his glory standing forth from the gospel, *and* our seeing him for who he is. The treasure is both the glory of Christ and the miracle of knowing him as gloriously present in our hearts.

It is not strange that Paul would use the word *treasure* to describe the glory of Christ in the human heart. Nothing would be more natural for Paul. He loves to think of Christ as the believer's wealth, his riches, his treasure. He speaks of the "unsearchable riches of Christ" (Eph. 3:8), God's "riches in glory in Christ Jesus" (Phil. 4:19), "the immeasurable riches of his grace in kindness toward us in Christ Jesus" (Eph. 2:7), and "the riches of the glory of this mystery, which is Christ in you, the hope of glory" (Col. 1:27). This was the heartbeat of his ministry, the meaning of his life. He saw himself "as poor, yet making many rich" (2 Cor. 6:10)—rich with Christ!

What this means for our question, then, is that 2 Corinthians 4:6 describes the way a believer comes into being, that is, the way *saving faith* comes into being. It happens when God removes spiritual blindness and replaces it with a sight of the glory of God in Christ—the beauty of Christ, the worth of Christ, the divine reality of Christ. This miracle of spiritual sight is believing. That is, it is the receiving of Christ as true and glorious. In this miracle, the believer is simultaneously united to Christ. We "have" Christ. He is ours and we are his. Then to make things crystal clear, Paul calls this a "treasure" (2 Cor. 4:7).

Receive Him in All His Excellencies

I conclude, therefore, that saving faith for Paul is seeing and receiving Christ as our supreme treasure. It is more than this. But it is not less. John Owen, with his refreshing old-fashioned language, turns this understanding of saving faith into an urgent plea:

> This it is to *receive* the Lord Jesus in his comeliness and eminency. Let believers exercise their hearts abundantly unto this thing. . . . *Let us receive him in all his excellencies*, as he bestows himself upon us;—be frequent in thoughts of *faith*, comparing him with other beloveds, sin, world, legal righteousness; and *preferring him before them*, counting them all loss and dung in comparison of him.[1]

To have saving faith in Christ is to *see* his excellencies as superior to all the world. To *prefer him* before all the world. To *receive* him as better than all the world. To *welcome* him in his "comeliness and eminency" as our supreme treasure.

---

1 John Owen, *Of Communion with God the Father, Son, and Holy Ghost*, vol. 2, *The Works of John Owen*, ed. William H. Goold (Edinburgh: T&T Clark, n.d.), 59; emphasis added.

How Moses Was Freed from the Treasures of Egypt

We've been focusing mainly on the "treasure" language of 2 Corinthians 4:7. By way of broadening our biblical foundation for treasuring Christ, I turn briefly to Hebrews 11:24–27. We looked at this text in chapter 10 as a partial exposition of Hebrews 11:1 to show that saving faith is the real, present experience of the future realities that God has promised. But we did not focus on faith as receiving Christ as our supreme treasure. That's what we focus on now:

> By faith Moses, when he was grown up, refused to be called the son of Pharaoh's daughter, choosing rather to be mistreated with the people of God than to enjoy the fleeting pleasures of sin. He considered the reproach of Christ greater wealth than the treasures of Egypt, for he was looking to the reward. By faith he left Egypt, not being afraid of the anger of the king, for he endured as seeing him who is invisible. (Heb. 11:24–27)

This text describes the inner workings of the experience of faith. I say "inner workings" because most of what happens in this text is inside Moses's mind and heart: *refused, choosing, enjoy, considered, looking, unafraid, seeing.* And since verses 24 and 27 begin with "By faith," it is fair to say that the writer's aim is to describe for us what faith looks like as an experience of the mind and heart.

Roots of Moses's Liberation

The argument of these verses is developed in four steps. We can describe the argument from the final outcome backward and downward into its foundations, moving step by step from one support to the next one under it.

1. Negatively stated, Moses refused the fleeting pleasures of Egypt and the privileges of being called the son of Pharaoh's daughter. Positively stated, Moses chose instead to be mistreated with the people of God (Heb. 11:24–25).

   2. The ground of this refusing and choosing was the peculiarly high estimate Moses put on the value of the reproach of Christ (which means "Messiah"). He estimated it as greater wealth than the treasures of Egypt (11:26a).

      3. The ground of this estimate of the reproach of Christ was that Moses looked to the reward (11:26b).

      4. The specific nature or content of the reward was Christ himself, seen by Moses as the unseen one (11:27).

All of this is a description of the inner workings of faith. It is the way faith has influence and produces its effects in our lives. What is the relationship in this text between faith and the receiving of Christ as our supreme treasure?

We see the answer as we restate the argument, working our way in reverse this time from the bottom support to the top effect. I put steps 3 and 4 on the same margin because step 4 is not a support for step 3 but a definition of it. In step 3, Moses is "looking to the reward." In step 4, that act is described as "seeing him who is invisible." Who is "him who is invisible"? The fact that Moses had just referred to the Messiah (11:26) makes it likely that this is who he has in mind. In the New Testament, the Greek word for "Christ" (*christos*) is used as both a proper name and a title, namely, Messiah.

So, putting steps 3 and 4 together, what we see is that Moses was looking to the unseen Christ as his great reward. This is the fundamental act of faith. He "greeted" the Messiah from afar (Heb. 11:13). That is, he welcomed him. He reached out, as it were, with the arms of faith and embraced Christ as his great reward.

Then steps 3 and 4 together support step 2. Seeing and greeting and embracing Christ as his great reward, Moses experienced the substance of this hoped-for Christ as a present reality. This present experience was so compelling to Moses that it caused the enjoyments of sin to fade in comparison to the value of joining Christ in his reproach.

He Tasted the Substance of the Hoped-For Christ

This is an illustration of Hebrews 11:1: "Faith is the substance of things hoped for" (KJV). Moses hoped for Christ as his great reward. Therefore, faith was the substance of that. Faith was the essential, present experience of Christ as a great reward. And that present experience turned the pleasure of sin into displeasure, and the pain of reproach into gain. Step 1 was the fruit of this faith—the choices Moses made for how to act. He renounced privilege and moved toward mistreatment.

So my conclusion from Hebrews 11:24–27 is that saving faith looks to him who is invisible—namely, Christ—and sees him as a great reward. Faith perceives the pleasures of Christ as greater than the pleasures of sin and privilege. And faith receives him as a supreme treasure.

Turning to the Decisive Point

The main point of part 3 has been to show that saving faith is not less than a receiving of Christ as our supreme treasure. It involves more, but not less. The emphasis has not fallen on the affectional act of the heart in actually treasuring Christ, though I have not been able to hide the explosive point that this is implied. But now we turn in part 4 to make that implication explicit.

PART 4

CHRIST, THE BELIEVER'S TREASURE AND SATISFACTION

We come now to the most essential question: If saving faith is not only a receiving of Christ, but also a receiving of him as our supreme treasure, does this kind of receiving determine and shape the nature of faith? We posed this question at the end of chapter 12 by referring to John Owen's claim that

> faith brings into the soul an experience of [the] power and efficacy [of the unseen things that are believed], whereby [the soul] is cast into the mold of them, or made conformable unto them.[1]

---

1   John Owen, *An Exposition of the Epistle to the Hebrews*, vol. 24, *The Works of John Owen*, ed. William H. Goold (Edinburgh: Johnstone & Hunter, 1854), 12.

Is that true? On the face of it, the answer seems obvious. If we receive Christ as a *treasure*, is not then the nature of faith *treasuring*? If we receive Christ as a *joy*, is not then the nature of faith *enjoyment*? If we receive Christ as *satisfying*, is not then the nature of faith *satisfaction*? And, of course, all these affectional dimensions of saving faith are *in Christ*. Saving faith is not treasuring and enjoying and being satisfied generically, as if the affectional experience had value in itself. No. Saving faith in all its dimensions is always a receiving of *Christ*. We receive satisfaction. We receive enjoyment. We receive the treasure. All of this receiving is receiving Christ.

It also seems obvious from another angle that receiving Christ as a treasure would imply that the nature of saving faith includes the affectional dimension of treasuring Christ. I argued in chapter 12 that saving faith is a supernatural creation by God, and is, therefore, supernaturally different from any faith that demons or man can have apart from a supernatural new birth. From this angle, it follows that the nature of this new creation is given by the way God creates faith.

I argued from 2 Corinthians 4:6 that God brings a believer into existence by creating in a person an experience of Christ as who he really is—namely, supremely glorious. God gives "the light of the knowledge of the glory of God in the face of Jesus Christ." Which is to say, God creates the experience of saving faith. When an unbeliever ceases to be an unbeliever, it is *not* Christ who has changed. What has changed is the nature of a person's experience of Christ. We were blind to his beauty and worth, but now we see and receive him as beautiful and worthy—as our supreme treasure.

The very fact that God created this experience—namely, saving faith—makes it obvious that the nature of the experience—the nature of saving faith—is determined by the beauty and value of

Christ. God's aim in bringing saving faith into existence is that we might receive Christ as our treasure. Therefore, he creates faith with that nature. Its nature is to see and treasure the glory of Christ. Is it not implausible that God would design and bring about a kind of faith that receives Christ as a treasure but does not treasure him? Therefore, the very fact that saving faith is a divine gift implies that its nature includes the affectional dimension of treasuring Christ. This is how God designs for his Son to be received.

But it is one thing to say that the very nature of the case makes it seem obvious that saving faith has affectional dimensions—like treasuring, enjoying, and being satisfied. It is another thing—which is even more compelling—to see in actual biblical texts how the affectional dimensions of saving faith are expressed. That's what part 4 aims to do.

17

Saving Faith Is the Substance
of Hoped-For Joy

IN CHAPTERS 10 AND 16, we began to press into the nature of saving faith as presented in the epistle to the Hebrews. In chapter 10, we focused on the word *substance* in Hebrews 11:1 and its implication for saving faith as the present experience of hoped-for reality. At the end of chapter 16, we pressed further into Moses's faith in Hebrews 11:24–27 as he embraced a greater treasure than the treasures of Egypt. In this chapter, we will walk over some of the same ground, but here the aim is to press through the general implications of the word *substance*, and through Moses's sight of a better treasure, to the question, What does Hebrews tell us about the affectional nature of faith itself?

We saw that the closest thing we have in Hebrews to a definition of faith is Hebrews 11:1. I have translated it (following the KJV), "Now faith is the substance of things hoped for, the evidence of things not seen." In chapter 10, I argued that the word *substance* (ὑπόστασις, *hupostasis*) in this verse means that faith is a present experience (a taste of the reality) of the future things that God has promised, especially the glory and worth of Christ.

Probing further into the way faith works in the book of Hebrews, we will find that the writer draws attention specifically to *joy* or *pleasure* as the affectional dimension of faith, which gives it an extraordinary, transforming power in the present. He does this by describing the way faith works in the life of Jesus, Moses, and the early Christians.

We have already focused significant attention on how the author treats these three illustrations of faith. But up till now, our focus has been on the nature of faith as the present realization of future reality and as the receiving of Christ as a treasure, not on the specific affectional aspect of faith as the *enjoyment* of Christ as our supreme treasure. This aspect has been implicit, but now I want to make it explicit.

Looking to Jesus

The writer of Hebrews presents Jesus in 12:1–3 as the "founder and perfecter" of our faith. This *founding* (ἀρχηγὸν, *archēgon*) includes not only Jesus's role as foundation, but also his role as illustration. He has not only secured our finishing the race victoriously (7:25); he has also run the race before us to show us how to do it. That's what Hebrews 12:1–3 is about.

The writer has just given in chapter 11 a litany of illustrations from the Old Testament of how to live by faith. The phrase *by faith* occurs nineteen times in Hebrews 11. Now, in Hebrews 12:1–3, the writer adds one more illustration of how to run the race with endurance *by faith*—namely, the illustration of Jesus. So he calls us to "[look] to Jesus" (12:2). Specifically, what he wants us to look at is the way Jesus "endured the cross"—namely, "for the joy that was set before him." In other words, Jesus is not only the *foundation* of our faith because he died for us on the cross, but also the *model* for our faith by the way he endured the cross.

Faith as Effectively Transformative

How did Jesus endure the cross? The writer wants us to see this so that we learn how to endure the hardships of the Christian life. "Consider him who endured from sinners such hostility against himself, so that you may not grow weary or fainthearted" (Heb. 12:3). So we "[look] to him" (v. 2) and "consider him" (v. 3). And what we are supposed to see is that Jesus was able to endure the horrors of the cross because he looked to "the joy that was set before him" (v. 2). Jesus looked beyond the cross and resurrection and saw everything God had planned from eternity for Jesus's glorification and for our salvation. The joy of this sight is what sustained him in the greatest act of love ever performed.

But how does that work psychologically? That is, how does a *future* joy become a powerful force in the *present* to overcome the human impulses to escape pain and crave relief? The answer given by the writer to the Hebrews is in the first verse of chapter 11—a chapter about the transformative effectiveness of faith. He said, "Faith is the substance of things hoped for." The reason I say that Hebrews 11 is about the *transformative effectiveness* of faith is that nineteen times in this chapter the writer attributes to faith the effective power of what the Old Testament heroes were able to do.

"By faith" is the effective way that Abraham obeyed (11:8). "By faith" is the effective way that others

suffered mocking and flogging, and even chains and imprisonment. They were stoned, they were sawn in two, they were killed with the sword. They went about in skins of sheep and goats, destitute, afflicted, mistreated—of whom the world was not worthy—wandering about in deserts and mountains, and in dens and caves of the earth. And all these, though commended *through their faith* . . . (Heb. 11:36–39)

Future Joy Experienced Now in "Substance" by Faith

Jesus is given in Hebrews 12:2 as the climactic illustration of one "of whom the world was not worthy," but who endured in love "by faith." In the case of Jesus, the truth that he endured the cross "by faith" is stated like this: "For the joy that was set before him [he] endured the cross." This future joy had present, obedience-sustaining power (Heb. 5:8), because of the truth of Hebrews 11:1: "Faith is the substance of things hoped for."

When Jesus saw, with the eye of faith, the joy on the other side of the resurrection, he experienced some measure of this joy in the present by faith. Its *substance* was not merely future. It was realized in the present. The word *realized* is a more familiar way of saying *substantialized*—a word nobody uses but that echoes the word *substance* in Hebrews 11:1. The reality of the "thing hoped for" was tasted by Jesus in the present. It was present in his faith. Faith is the present experience of the substance of things hoped for. This is how a future, looked-for, hoped-for joy becomes a mighty force of love in the present. For no greater act of love was ever performed than when Jesus "endured the cross" to save his enemies.

What this means for our question is this: when we embrace a hoped-for joy by faith, that joy becomes a *substantial* element or dimension of our faith, because faith is the *substance* of things hoped for. For Jesus, this faith was the embrace of the hoped-for joy of his own infinitely deserved glorification, surrounded by redeemed saints and adoring angels. For us, this faith is the embrace of the hoped-for joy of sharing in the ill-deserved but graciously given glory of Christ, exalted in our eternal adoration.

The joy that is set before us in the promises of God becomes present and powerful in our faith. Faith sees the future, joyful reality in the promise of God and tastes the substance of it now. The substance of the future joy is brought back into the present. This is the affectional dimension of saving faith. Saving faith is *receiving* Christ as a treasure, which we now see means receiving Christ *enjoyed* as a treasure now. Because faith is the substance of the hoped-for, all-satisfying Christ.

Are Faith and Hope Different?

It may be helpful to include here a few reflections on the relationship between faith and hope. The way I have described faith, it sounds indistinguishable from hope—as when I say that faith sees the future, joyful reality in the promise of God and tastes the substance of it now. But faith and hope are not identical. This is obvious from the fact that faith can look to the past and believe that something really happened. For example, "If you . . . *believe* in your heart that God raised [Christ] from the dead . . ." (Rom. 10:9). Paul would never say, "If you *hope* in your heart that God raised him from the dead . . ." Hope is always future-oriented.

But faith is most often future-oriented—based on the past triumph of Christ in his death and resurrection, but focused on the promises of God for the next five minutes and the countless ages of eternity.[1] And this future orientation of faith overlaps with the meaning of hope, and they become almost indistinguishable. This

---

1 My book *Future Grace: The Purifying Power of the Promises of God*, rev. ed. (Colorado Springs, CO: Multnomah, 2012) is based on the conviction that this future orientation of faith, along

should not be a surprise when we realize that over fifty times in the Greek Old Testament the word for *hope* (ἐλπίζω, *elpizō*) is used to translate the Hebrew word for *trust* (בָּטַח, *batach*). For example, "Trust [ἔλπισον, *elpison*, hope] in the LORD, and do good" (Ps. 37:3). "O LORD of hosts, blessed is the one who trusts [ὁ ἐλπίζων, *ho elpizōn*, hopes] in you!" (Ps. 84:12).

As Paul uses the two terms (hope and faith), they are sometimes difficult to distinguish. See, for example, Romans 4:18: "In *hope* [Abraham] *believed* against *hope*, that he should become the father of many nations. . . . He did not weaken in *faith*. . . . No *unbelief* made him waver concerning the promise of God" (Rom. 4:18–20). Or Colossians 1:23: "Continue in . . . *faith*, stable and steadfast, not shifting from the *hope* of the gospel." Or Ephesians 1:12–13, where Paul refers to the Jews who were "the first to *hope* in Christ," and then to the Gentiles like this: "You *also* . . . *believed* in [Christ]." Or the benediction of Romans 15:13: "May the God of *hope* fill you with all joy and peace in *believing*, so that by the power of the Holy Spirit you may abound in *hope*."

But Hebrews 11:1 ("Now *faith* is the substance of things *hoped* for") gives us the most precise statement of the relationship between faith and hope. I would state it like this: when hope for something that God has promised becomes an experienced, present taste and power of the reality hoped for, we may also call it *faith*.

Moses's Experience of Hoped-For Wealth and Pleasure

As we move from the example of Jesus to the example of Moses in Hebrews 11:24–27, we see the same point—namely, saving faith is *receiving* Christ as an *enjoyed* treasure now, because faith is the

---

with the affectional nature of faith, is why faith inevitably severs the root of sin's deceptive promises and bears the fruit of love.

substance of the hoped-for, all-satisfying Christ. We already dealt with this passage in detail in chapter 16. So we will make just one thing explicit here that was implicit there. An essential element of Moses's faith was the realization in the present of the substance of a hoped-for future joy. In other words, the writer of Hebrews gives Moses as another illustration of how faith is the substance of things hoped for (11:1), and how joy or pleasure is the specific affection that faith *substantializes* (experiences as substantially real) in the present:

> By faith Moses, when he was grown up, refused to be called the son of Pharaoh's daughter, choosing rather to be mistreated with the people of God than to enjoy the fleeting pleasures of sin. He considered the reproach of Christ greater wealth than the treasures of Egypt, for he was looking to the reward. By faith he left Egypt, not being afraid of the anger of the king, for he endured as seeing him who is invisible. (Heb. 11:24–27)

In the same way that Jesus looked to "the joy . . . set before him" (Heb. 12:2) and was able to endure the cross, so Moses "looked to the reward" and was able to endure the "reproach of Christ." But now we can draw attention more specifically to how this "looking to the reward" became so powerful in Moses's present experience. When Moses saw the greatness of the reward of Christ ("seeing him who is invisible," 11:27), his faith became the "substance of things hoped for."

And the nature of that experienced substance in Moses's life was both a kind of "wealth" and a kind of "pleasure." He embraced the reproach of Christ as "greater *wealth* than the treasure of Egypt." And he embraced mistreatment with God's people as preferable to the "fleeting *pleasures* of sin." Calling the pleasures of sin *fleeting* implies that there is a better kind. There are pleasures that last forever (Ps. 16:11). They are the pleasures of the reward of "him who is invisible."

This double realization of wealth and pleasure, by which Moses was so radically changed, is faith. "By faith" (Heb. 11:24, 27) Moses looked to the reward. "By faith" Moses considered reproach to be wealth. "By faith" Moses preferred long-term pleasures with the unseen Messiah over the fleeting pleasures of sin. In other words, faith was the substance of things hoped for. Faith was the present experience of the substance of the reward, the substance of the wealth, the substance of the pleasures. In faith Moses tasted the all-satisfying Christ.

Christians Loved by Means of Realized Joy

Now we look once more at the faith of the early Christians of Hebrews 10:32–35. Their experience confirms how faith as "the substance of things hoped for" (11:1) takes the form of joy:

> Recall the former days when, after you were enlightened, you endured a hard struggle with sufferings, sometimes being publicly exposed to reproach and affliction, and sometimes being partners with those so treated. For you had compassion on those in prison, and you *joyfully* [μετὰ χαρᾶς, *meta charas*] accepted the plundering of your property, since you knew that you yourselves had a better possession and an abiding one. Therefore do not throw away your confidence, which has a great reward. (Heb. 10:32–35)

Like Moses in Hebrews 11:24–27 and Jesus in Hebrews 12:1–3, the Christians of Hebrews 10:34 are able to endure suffering be-

cause they look to the "better possession and . . . abiding one."
Jesus looked to the "joy . . . set before him" (12:2). Moses looked
to the "reward" (11:26). The Christians look to a future that is
better and eternal. How did these "things hoped for" become
real and effective ("substance") in their present experience? How
could these Christians not only *risk* the loss of their property in
showing compassion to imprisoned believers, but actually *lose* their
property? The answer is that they had such a sight of their future
reward that they were able to lose their possessions "with joy" (μετὰ
χαρᾶς, *meta charas*).

The experience of joy released them from fear and selfishness,
and compelled compassion. And what was that joy? Where did it
come from? It was the substance of things hoped for (11:1). The
source of their sacrificial love was this: "Since you knew that you
yourselves had a better possession and an abiding one" (10:34).
This was the future they put their hope in when they pondered
risking their lives for the sake of their brothers. And this joyful
future flowed back into the present and became real, substantial,
powerfully effective. It was the arrival in advance of real joy, future
joy, experienced now. Hebrews calls that experience *faith*. "Faith is
the substance of things hoped for." And the affectional dimension
of this faith is joy. When faith embraces the treasure of a joyful
future—a "better possession and an abiding one"—the faith itself
becomes the present substance, the taste, of that future joy.

Without This Faith, We Are Not Saved

Make no mistake: we are talking here about *saving* faith. The embrace of a better and abiding future is what we experience when
we are savingly converted. The last verse of this unit puts the spot-
light on this fact: "Therefore do not throw away your confidence

[παρρησίαν, *parrēsian*], which has a great reward" (Heb. 10:35). Losing this great "reward" (the same word for the "reward" that Moses looked for in 11:26), is not the loss of choice real estate in heaven. It's the loss of heaven. If you lose your "confidence" (finally and decisively), you lose Christ.

The writer puts it like this in Hebrews 3:6: "We are [God's] house, if indeed we hold fast our confidence [παρρησίαν, *parrēsian*] and our boasting in our hope." This is how we began the Christian life, and this is how we persevere—by confidence, that is, by faith in the superiority of Christ and all God promises to be for us in him.

Then, eight verses later (3:14), the author explicitly connects this point with the word *substance* in Hebrews 11:1. He clarifies that losing confidence finally and decisively (apostasy) does not mean we lose union with Christ, but that we never had it. He says in Hebrews 3:14, "We have come to share in Christ [union with Christ], if indeed we hold our original confidence [substance, ὑποστάσεως, *hupostaseōs*] firm to the end." Future perseverance in faith confirms the past reality of faith.

This same point was made in Hebrews 3:6: "We are [Christ's] house, if indeed we hold fast our confidence and our boasting in our hope." The word that the ESV translates as *confidence* in Hebrews 3:14 (ὑποστάσεως, *hupostaseōs*), and the word translated *confidence* in Hebrews 3:6 (παρρησίαν, *parrēsian*), are not the same. But they are functioning in essentially the same way: If we don't hold fast our confidence in verse 6, we are not God's house. If we don't hold fast our confidence in verse 14, we have never been united to Christ. The point is essentially the same.

But there's a difference. *Confidence* (παρρησίαν, *parrēsian*) in Hebrews 3:6 connects to the same word in Hebrews 10:35 and confirms that the author is talking about *saving* faith when he says,

"Do not throw away your *confidence* [παρρησίαν, *parrēsian*], which has a great reward [of final salvation]." But *confidence* in Hebrews 3:14 connects to the word *substance* (ὑποστάσεως, *hupostaseōs*) in Hebrews 11:1 and confirms that we are talking about *faith*. "Faith is the *substance* of things hoped for."

I conclude, therefore, from these three passages in Hebrews (12:1–3; 11:24–27; 10:32–35), together with the lynchpin of Hebrews 11:1, that saving faith contains the affectional dimension of joyfully receiving Christ as our treasure.

Joy Is in the Nature of the Receiving

It is not insignificant that the very phrase *with joy* in Hebrews 10:34 is also used in 1 Thessalonians 1:6 as the way the Thessalonians received the gospel. Paul saw this receiving with joy as evidence of their election. "We know, brothers loved by God, that he has chosen you, because . . . you received the word in much affliction, *with* . . . *joy* [μετὰ χαρᾶς, *meta charas*, as in Hebrews 10:34]" (1 Thess. 1:4–6).

Paul saw this as one evidence that his preaching of Christ was having a real, saving effect. We may infer that saving faith is not receiving *plus* joy, any more than the object of faith is Christ *plus* treasure. Christ *is* the treasure we receive. And joy is included in the nature of the receiving.

Saving faith does not receive Christ as disappointing. It does not receive Christ as boring, or foolish, or inferior, or secondary, or ugly, or undesirable. Saving faith receives Christ as he really is. Not that we know the totality of his greatness at the beginning of our relationship. But given what we do know, we see him as supremely desirable. No one could be a greater source of joy than Christ. Saving faith tastes this (realizes this substance) and receives Christ as such—with joy.

18

Saving Faith as Love for the Truth of the Gospel

IN 2 THESSALONIANS 2, Paul is dealing with the end-time coming of "the man of lawlessness" and a great apostasy among professing believers (v. 3). He wants to help the church not be deceived. So he describes how deception happens:

> The coming of the lawless one is by the activity of Satan with all power and lying signs and wonders, and with all wicked deception for those who are perishing, because they did not receive [ἐδέξαντο, *edexanto*] the love of the truth in order to be saved. Therefore God sends them a strong delusion, so that they may believe what is false, in order that all may be condemned who did not believe the truth but had pleasure in unrighteousness. (2 Thess. 2:9–12, my translation)

There are several very striking things here. The two that I want us to focus on are (1) the clause "did not receive the love of the truth," and (2) the contrast between "not [believing] the truth but [having] pleasure in unrighteousness." Both of these point to the affectional nature of saving faith.

Not Loving the Truth and Not Believing the Truth

First, Paul says that people are "perishing because they did not receive [welcome] the love of the truth in order to be saved." The *truth* here is the gospel message Paul preached. In 2 Thessalonians 2:13, Paul says, "God chose you . . . for salvation by . . . *faith in the truth*" (my translation)—that is, by faith in the gospel of Christ, which he calls "the truth." So when Paul says in 2 Thessalonians 2:10 that people fail to be saved because they refuse to welcome "the love of the truth," we should see a close relationship between loving the truth and believing.

Loving the truth and believing the truth are linked in another way. In 2:10, people perish because they do not "love the truth." And in 2:12, people are condemned because they do not "believe the truth." Since failing to love the truth and failing to believe the truth both bring judgment, Paul does not appear to be making any distinction between them.

But what's really striking in these words is Paul's statement that they did not "receive" a love for the truth, and that is why they are "perishing" and are not "saved." He could have simply said, "They are perishing because they did not love the truth." But instead he said, "They are perishing because they did not *receive* [or *welcome*] the love of the truth." What does that mean?

Deep Resistance to Even Being Helped to Love the Truth

Behind this description of the human condition is Paul's conviction that the human heart is not neutral. It is not simply marked by the *absence* of love for the truth. It is marked by *resistance* to love for the truth. Paul knows that if any fallen human being is going to love the truth of the gospel, that love will have to be a gift. It will have to be *received*. It will never arise from the spiritual deadness that marks all people (Eph. 2:1–3).

So Paul is saying that people perish not only because they do not love the truth, but also because they do not *want* to love the truth. And this is seen in the fact that they do not want any help in loving the truth. If the love of truth were offered to them as a gift, they would not take it. So this is deeper than not loving the truth. This is not *wanting* to love the truth. This is a contrary love, that is, a love of untruth. This is why people will be deceived so readily by "false signs and wonders" (2 Thess. 2:9). People are already deeply committed to falsehood.

What does this tell us about saving faith? Paul makes the connection explicit. In verse 13, we are saved by "*belief* in the truth." In verse 10, we perish for our deep resistance to a "*love* of the truth." Does it not seem, then, that saving faith includes a miraculous work of God by which our deep resistance to the truth is replaced with a love for the truth, the gospel? And would not this awakening of love for the truth be simultaneous with, and inseparable from, belief in the truth? And since both are said to save, would it not be right to say that *saving faith* includes a *love* for the truth, the gospel? And would not this love be an affectional dimension of saving faith?

Saving Faith Does Not Find Superior Pleasure in Unrighteousness

This conclusion is confirmed in Paul's second striking statement in 2 Thessalonians 2:12. All are "condemned who did not believe the truth but had pleasure [εὐδοκήσαντες, *eudokēsantes*] in unrighteousness." This is a surprising contrast. It's not what we expect. He does not contrast believing in the truth with believing in falsehood. He contrasts believing in the truth with *taking pleasure in unrighteousness.* In other words, one way to describe the alternative to saving faith is this: taking greater pleasure in sin.

So Paul again, as in verse 10, calls attention to the affectional nature of saving faith. It includes a *love* of the truth, the gospel. Or, as verse 12 suggests, it includes taking greater *pleasure* in the gospel than in unrighteousness. Therefore, saving faith is a receiving of Christ not only as true, but also as better than the pleasures of sin, and therefore as loved, cherished, preferred, treasured above alternative sources of pleasure.

How Not to Believe in Lying Signs and Wonders

Linger with me for a few moments over the implications of what we have just seen in 2 Thessalonians. One implication is that when "false signs and wonders" are performed by false prophets (2 Thess. 2:9), our "love of the truth" is being tested. People perish "because they refused to *love the truth*" (2:10). Love of the truth would have kept them from being deceived and perishing. Or to say it more comprehensively, what is being tested is our *faith* in Christ, but especially that dimension of faith that consists in *love* of the truth of the gospel of Christ.

Why is this worth lingering over? First, because it is a peculiar insight: *love* for the truth, not just *knowledge* of the truth or *belief* in the truth, enables us to see through the deceitfulness of lying signs and wonders. We don't usually think of love as a faculty of discernment. Discernment is what *knowledge* does. And firm *faith* in true facts can keep us from being misled. But without denying that, Paul adds something crucial to our understanding. *Love* for the truth of the gospel—love for the Christ of the gospel and all that God is for us in him—is indeed a discerning faculty. When we don't have it, we will be prey to lying signs and wonders.

Love for Christ, an Indispensable Faculty of Discernment

What does it mean that love is a discerning faculty? Love for the truth of the gospel of Christ means that the soul sees and embraces Christ in the gospel as he really is, not as deceitful wonder workers present him. Those who have love for the truth see Christ as *divinely beautiful* and *great* and *valuable* and *pleasing*.

Each of those five words is important for describing how love beholds and embraces Christ. I say *divinely* because all of these traits are given by God and carry the marks of his divinity. I say *beautiful* because it sums up the perfect fullness and proportion of Christ's moral excellencies. I say *great* because, on the scale of magnificence and grandeur, none surpasses him. I say *valuable* because, on the scale of worth, he exceeds all others. And I say *pleasing* because this is how love receives such divine beauty and greatness and worth. They please the soul.

So love for Christ sees in the gospel what is really there (2 Cor. 4:6). Others who do not have this love do not see it. That is, love sees Christ in the gospel as *divine*. Love sees Christ in the gospel as *beautiful*. Love sees Christ in the gospel as *great* and *valuable* and *pleasing*. This seeing is not neutral. It's not as though love to Christ could see Christ this way, and then stand there neutral, contemplating whether to feel pleased or not. Being pleased by the glories of Christ is not a choice from a position of indifference. To see divine glory in Christ, as he really is, is to love him, to be pleased with him.

This is why love for the truth of the gospel protects us from lying signs and wonders. When a lying sign and wonder calls us to turn from Christ and embrace another, love rises up and says, "No! Why would I do that? I have seen his divine glory. It is pleasing to the soul. I am satisfied with his superior beauty and greatness and value. You cannot lure me away from what I see and savor with such satisfaction." That is the language of love. And that is the power of discernment against lying signs and wonders.

Jesus and Moses Point to the Same Protection from Deception

Now, here is the second reason for lingering over these implications of 2 Thessalonians 2. Just as Paul treats this "love of the truth" as an essential dimension of saving faith, so Jesus's warnings about lying signs and wonders, and Moses's warnings about lying signs and wonders, lead to the same conclusion. Recall that Paul contrasted saving faith with "pleasure in unrighteousness." People are "condemned who did not believe the truth but had pleasure in unrighteousness" (2 Thess. 2:12). This contrast makes sense because saving faith includes having pleasure in Christ— that is, loving Christ. Therefore, saving faith consists not only in the confidence we have about the facts of Christ, but also in the love we feel for the beauty of Christ. Unbelief has "pleasure in unrighteousness." Belief has a superior pleasure in the truth of Christ. Therefore, love for Christ is an essential dimension of saving faith.

Jesus dealt with lying signs and wonders in terms of *faith*. Moses dealt with lying signs and wonders in terms of *love*. And I am suggesting that Paul saw to the bottom of what they were doing and wove the two together—faith and love as one way of receiving Christ.

For example, in Matthew 24:23–27, Jesus warned about the kind of deception and testing Paul describes in 2 Thessalonians 2:

Then if anyone says to you, "Look, here is the Christ!" or "There he is!" do not believe [it]. For false christs and false prophets will arise and perform great signs and wonders, so as to lead astray, if possible, even the elect. See, I have told you beforehand. So, if they say to you, "Look, he is in the wilderness," do not go out. If they say, "Look, he is in the inner rooms," do not believe [it]. For as the lightning comes from the east and shines as far as the west, so will be the coming of the Son of Man. (Matt. 24:23–27)

The reason I put brackets around the word *it* in verses 23 and 26 is that the word is not there in the original Greek, and because the absence of any direct object makes Jesus's prohibition more comprehensive: Don't believe like this. Don't become that kind of believer. Don't give your belief over to another. Don't find the "false christs" and the "false prophets" as attractive as Christ. Don't see them as worthy of your belief!

Verse 27 gives a help to our faith: if you start to feel that the false christs are greater or more to be desired than Christ, remember that he is going to light up the sky from horizon to horizon, so that the flickering falsehood of these attractive little christs will vanish like a street light at bright midday. Don't let your faith be deceived. The signs and wonders that the false prophets perform are not more glorious than Christ in his coming. Don't be attracted! Don't be pleased by them! Don't find satisfaction in the lying glitz of signs and wonders. Stay with the glory of the sky-splitting, sky-filling Christ.

Or we could reach back to Matthew 24:11–13 and put this warning in terms of love. "Many false prophets will arise and lead many astray. And because lawlessness will be increased, the *love* of many will grow cold. But the one who endures to the end will be saved." *Cold love* toward Christ goes hand in hand with being led astray by the false prophets. Jesus does not make the connection between warm love and deception-avoiding faith as explicit as Paul does in 2 Thessalonians, but the pointers are there. Growing cold in love and being deceived by lawlessness and false prophets are linked (Matthew 24:11–12). And a failure of faith opens one to deception (Matt. 24:23, 26).

The Discerning Power of Love in the Teaching of Moses

Behind Paul's and Jesus's treatment of lying signs and wonders is the amazing way Moses deals with this same problem. What makes it amazing is that he shows that love for God is both what is being tested by false prophets and how the test is passed. The key passage is Deuteronomy 13:1–3:

> If a prophet or a dreamer of dreams arises among you and gives you a sign or a wonder, and the sign or wonder that he tells you comes to pass, and if he says, "Let us go after other gods," which you have not known, "and let us serve them," you shall not listen to the words of that prophet or that dreamer of dreams. For the Lord your God is testing you, to know whether you love the Lord your God with all your heart and with all your soul.

Notice five things:

1. Moses tells us that signs and wonders in the service of heresy really do happen. They are not tricks. "If a prophet . . . gives you a sign or a wonder, *and the sign or wonder that he tells you comes*

to pass . . ." In this case, the sign or wonder is a prediction about the future. And it really comes true. One can easily imagine the kind of popular following a person would get if he could predict what would happen tomorrow or a year from now. That's what some false prophets can do, Moses says.

2. Some miracle workers aim to draw believers away from the true God. "If he says, *'Let us go after other gods,'* . . . you shall not listen to the words of that prophet." So the lying supernatural signs and wonders are designed in the mind of the false prophet to be a compelling apologetic for another god besides Yahweh.

3. God himself has a design in these deceptive signs and wonders. He tells us what the design is: *"For the* LORD *your God is testing you,* to know whether you love the LORD your God with all your heart and with all your soul." When *temptation* happens from man, a *test* is happening from God. This is God's design in the deceptive signs and wonders.

4. Love for God is what God is testing. "Your God is testing you, *to know whether you love the* LORD *your God* with all your heart and with all your soul." He could have said that *faith* is being tested (as Jesus does in Matthew 24:23–27). But his focus remains on love to God.

5. Just as we saw in 2 Thessalonians 2:9–12, and just as Jesus hinted in Matthew 24:12, God treats love toward himself as a discerning faculty. Love for God sees through the deception of lying signs and wonders. This love is not based mainly on miraculous power. Otherwise, signs and wonders in the service

of a lie would be just as compelling as signs and wonders in the service of the truth. Love for God *sees through* miraculous power to the presence (or absence) of true divine beauty. Therefore, love for God, as in 2 Thessalonians 2:9–12, is a powerful protection against apostasy.

Saving Faith Is a Glad Reception of the Truth

What we have seen is that Moses, Jesus, and Paul deal with lying signs and wonders. Moses focuses on love for God. Love is what the false prophets want to destroy. And love has the discernment to protect us from destruction. Jesus focuses on belief in Christ. Belief is what the false prophets want to destroy. And belief is what holds fast to the sky-filling Christ. There is a hint in Matthew 24:12 that not letting our love grow cold is what it means to hold fast to Christ. Paul is the one who puts the pieces together in the fullest way. He treats love for Christ as an essential dimension of faith in Christ (2 Thess. 2:9–12). People perish for not receiving a *love* of the truth (2:9). People perish for not *believing* the truth (2:12). This is because love for Christ is an essential affectional aspect of saving faith. As Herman Witsius wrote:

> It is not possible but the believing soul, while in the exercise of faith, must sincerely *love* the truth as it is in Christ, when known and acknowledged, *rejoicing* that these things are true, and *delighting* itself in that truth: far otherwise than the devils and wicked men, who, what they know to be true, they could wish to be false.[1]

---

1   Herman Witsius, *The Economy of the Covenants between God and Man: Comprehending a Complete Body of Divinity*, trans. William Crookshank, vol. 1 (London: T. Tegg & Son, 1837), 345.

19

Saving Faith Overcomes the World

WE TURN NOW TO the writings of the apostle John and the way he weaves love for God and love for Christ together with saving faith. In this chapter, we will focus on John's first epistle, and in the next chapter on John's Gospel. Consider with me 1 John 5:1–5:

> Everyone who believes that Jesus is the Christ has been born of God, and everyone who loves the Father loves whoever has been born of him. By this we know that we love the children of God, when we love God and obey his commandments. For this is the love of God [i.e., this is what it means to love God], that we keep his commandments. And his commandments are not burdensome. For everyone who has been born of God overcomes the world. And this is the victory that has overcome the world—our faith. Who is it that overcomes the world except the one who believes that Jesus is the Son of God?

For Love, the Commandments Are Not Burdensome

Leaving aside many important questions about these verses, we cut to the chase and focus on the parts that connect love for God and faith in Christ. The key juncture is the connection between 1 John 5:3 and 5:4. The term "love of God" in verse 3 refers to our love for God, not his for us. We can see this because verse 2 says, "We know that we love the children of God, when *we love God*." So the "love of God" in verse 3 refers to that act of loving God in verse 2.

What then does he say in verse 3? He does not say that loving God consists merely in keeping his commandments, but that it consists in keeping his commandments *in such a way that they are not burdensome*. "This is the love of God, that we keep his commandments. And his commandments are not burdensome." The statement "his commandments are not burdensome" does not dangle as a marginal piece of information. It is essential to John's argument. It lies at the center of what it means to love God and have faith and overcome the world. We will see this shortly.

Overcoming the World Lifts the Burden of the Commandments

First John 5:4 is given as an argument, or a basis, for 5:3. We know this because verse 4 begins with *for* (or *because*): "*For* everyone who has been born of God overcomes the world. And this is the victory that has overcome the world—our faith." So verse 4 is given as an explanation for *why* obedience to God's commandments is not burdensome for born-again people. It is *because* born-again people "overcome the world."

How does that work? We need to know what John is thinking here when he says "world." How does the *world* hinder obedience to God by making obedience burdensome? The passage that takes us to the heart of the matter is 1 John 2:15–16:

> Do not love the world or the things in the world. If anyone loves the world, the love of the Father [i.e., love for the Father] is not in him. For all that is in the world—the desires of the flesh and the desires of the eyes and pride of life—is not from the Father but is from the world.

According to this text, what threatens our love for God is our love for the world. "If anyone loves the world, the love of the Father is not in him." So if we are to love God, we must "overcome" the world. The enslaving power of "the desires of the flesh and the desires of the eyes and the pride of life" (2:16) must be broken, overcome. Our loves must be liberated from slavery to the world. Before the new birth, they are bound to the things of this world, not to God. A mighty alteration needs to happen in our affections. Our preferences and pleasures and desires must shift from the world to God. Love of the world must become love for God. He, not the world, must become our pleasure and treasure.

New Birth Overcomes the World

Now back to 1 John 5:4. John says that this great alteration in what we desire and treasure comes about by being born again. "For everyone who has been born of God overcomes the world." The new birth is the origin of this great alteration from desiring the world to desiring God. And that alteration is called overcoming the world. The power of the world to hold our affections is broken in the miracle of new birth.

Therefore, the commandments of God no longer cut against the grain of our nature. Our nature is now a born-again nature. What made the commandments burdensome was our old nature that hated submission to God and loved the ego-exalting, flesh-feeding pleasures of the world. Paul put it like this: "The mind that is set on the flesh [the mindset that we have before new birth] is hostile to God, for it does not submit to God's law; indeed, it cannot. Those who are in the flesh cannot please God" (Rom. 8:7–8). But in the new birth, that rebellious bondage to the flesh and the world is overcome. Not only is the old addiction to the "the desires of the flesh and the desires of the eyes" broken, but new desires, new loves, are brought to life. Because of these, the commandments of God are now what we *want* to do, not just what we have to do. They cease to be burdensome.

Faith Is How We Experience New Birth— That Is, Overcoming the World

John adds in the second half of 1 John 5:4 that the sum of this amazing experience is *faith*. "For everyone who has been born of God overcomes the world. *And this is the victory that has overcome the world—our faith*." In other words, overcoming the world is given by God as *new birth*, and is experienced by us as *faith*. That's why 5:1 says, "Everyone who believes . . . has been born of God."

Therefore, what we have in 5:4 is an explanation of why the commandments of God are not burdensome. One way to say it is that we are born again. Another way to say it is that we have *faith*. Faith overcomes the world (5:4b). And the new birth overcomes the world (5:4a). It's the same experience viewed from two sides. Overcoming the world means overcoming the inclinations of our heart that make the commandments of God burdensome. Therefore, both the new birth and faith may be described as the way the commandments cease to be burdensome.

Now we are prepared to see the connection between this faith (in Jesus the Son of God, v. 5) and love for God. The connection is this: both love for God and faith in Christ are described as the way the commandments cease to be burdensome. Verse 3 puts it like this: "This is the *love of God*, that we keep his commandments. And *his commandments are not burdensome*." Verse 4 puts it like this: they are not burdensome "because . . . [faith] is the victory that overcomes the world." Faith dethrones the enslaving desires for the world and replaces the world with God in our affections. Which John also calls loving God.

So my conclusion from 1 John 5:1–5 is that, in the mind of John, saving faith includes the affectional dimension of loving God. First John 5:3–4 does not describe two distinct ways of overcoming the world and removing the burdensomeness of God's commandments. They describe one composite way using different language: love for God and faith in Christ.

I use the word *composite* so as not to overstate my conclusion. I am not saying that faith in Christ and love for God are *identical*. I am saying that saving faith is a composite of different ways that the born-again soul receives Christ. And one of those ways of receiving him is to receive him as superior to everything that makes God's commandments difficult. John calls this faith. And he calls it loving God.

I Do Not Insist That Edwards Is Entirely Right

I do not go so far as Jonathan Edwards in his conclusion from this text, though he may be right. Based on the connection between 1 John 5:3 and 5:4, Edwards concludes:

This [v. 4] is explaining what he had said before [v. 3], that our love to God enables us to overcome the difficulties that attend keeping God's commands; which shows that *love is the main thing in saving faith, the life and power of it*, by which it produces its great effects.[1]

In calling love to God "the main thing in saving faith," he is not denying any other biblical aspects or implications of faith. He does not reject the traditional explanation of faith as knowledge (*notitia*), assent (*assensus*), and trust (*fiducia*). Rather, he is trying to come to terms with biblical texts. When he calls love to God the main thing in saving faith, he has in view the "life and power" of faith to overcome the world and turn the commandments into blessed delight rather than burdensome duty, as the psalmist experienced: "I find my delight in your commandments, which I love" (Ps. 119:47). "I love your commandments above gold" (Ps. 119:127). "Your commandments are my delight" (Ps. 119:143).

Whether we should call this aspect of saving faith "the main thing in saving faith" is debatable. In view of 1 John 5:3–4, it is certainly a *powerful* thing in saving faith and goes a long way to explaining why the Westminster Confession says that justifying faith "is ever accompanied with all other saving graces, and is no dead faith, but works by love" (11.2).

---

1 Jonathan Edwards, *Writings on the Trinity, Grace, and Faith*, ed. Sang Hyun Lee and Harry S. Stout, vol. 21, *The Works of Jonathan Edwards* (New Haven, CT: Yale University Press, 2003), 448. As a lover of Jonathan Edwards, I nevertheless do not consider him above correction, both in his convictions and in his expressions. Readers should be aware that Edwards's way of articulating justification by faith alone is one of his most embattled positions. George Hunsinger ("Dispositional Soteriology: Jonathan Edwards on Justification by Faith Alone" in *Westminster Theological Journal*, vol. 66, no. 1 [2004]); J. V. Fesko (*Justification: Considering the Classic Reformed Doctrine* [Phillipsburg, NJ: P&R, 2008]); and others have criticized Edwards's view, or at least his articulation of it, as out of sync with historic Reformed teaching.

Edwards is saying (and in this I do agree) that the reason justifying faith has this extraordinary effect of *always* producing the fruit of holiness (Heb. 12:14) is not only that those who are justified by faith have been born again and receive the Holy Spirit, but also that justifying faith is itself of such a nature as to overcome the world's desire for sin and transform heavy commandments into happy corridors of obedience. And it does so because in it is love for God as supremely valuable and satisfying.

20

Whoever Believes in Me
Shall Never Thirst

TURNING NOW TO John's Gospel, we find the most sustained focus on believing in the whole Bible—the kind of believing that comes with eternal life. Here we find the more straightforward statements about the affectional dimensions of believing than we find anywhere else in the Bible. Astonishingly, the noun for *belief* or *faith* (same word in Greek, πίστις, *pistis*) does not occur in John's Gospel. Instead, the verb for *believing* or *having faith* (πιστεύω, *pisteuō*) occurs ninety-eight times.

John's Love for the Verb *Believe*

I do not know with certainty what John was trying to tell us by this remarkable choice of the verb over the noun, which could hardly have been accidental. We have seen that he is happy to use the noun *faith* in 1 John 5:4: "This is the victory that has overcome the world—our faith [πίστις, *pistis*]"—the only use of the noun *faith* in all his writings.[1]

---

1 I believe the author of the Gospel of John and the author of the epistles of John is the same person. That is the tradition of the church, the consensus of evangelical

But in what follows, I will venture a guess about John's reason for only using the verb *believe*, and never using the noun *faith*.

Sometimes a biblical writer uses words in a way that we cannot fully explain, and yet that God knows will have a good effect on us. What is crucial in dealing with John's language of "believing" is not that we can explain fully why he preferred the verb, but that we dig deeply into what he does with the verb when he uses it.

Believing as Receiving

We have noted more than once (chapters 7 and 12) how central *receiving Christ* is to the nature of saving faith. This is true not only for Paul ("As you *received* Christ Jesus the Lord, so walk in him," Col. 2:6), but also for John (1:12; 5:43; 6:21; 12:48; 13:20). John shows us that *receiving* Christ and *believing* Christ are two dimensions of one experience. They need not be exhaustively identical, but they are used interchangeably in John 1:12:

> [Jesus] came to his own, and his own people did not receive him. But to all who did *receive* him, who *believed* in his name, he gave the right to become children of God, who were born, not of blood nor of the will of the flesh nor of the will of man, but of God. (John 1:11–13)

The question we are asking in this chapter is how John's other more affectional descriptions of believing fit together with his understanding of believing as receiving.

---

scholarship, and, most importantly, confirmed by a strong similarity in language, style, and conceptuality.

John's Broad, Absolute Use of "Believe"

For my purposes, it is not essential to go into any detail about the various words John uses to connect believing with what or who is believed—for example, when *pisteuō* ("I believe") is followed by the pronoun *eis* ("in," over thirty times, e.g., 1:50; 3:12; 4:41), or by *en* ("in," 3:15), or by objects in the dative (5:24; 6:30) or in the accusative (11:26), or by a clause introduced by *hoti* ("that," 8:24). What I will try to show is that across all of John's references to believing, none is saving that does not include the affectional dimension of believing.

There are reasons for thinking broadly about *believing* in the Gospel of John—that is, thinking about a meaning for *believing* that covers a broad range of uses. For example, it is striking how frequently (some eighteen times), he refers to *believing* with no object whatsoever. Just an absolute use, such as "You do not *believe* because you are not among my sheep" (10:26). Or: "Many more *believed* because of his word" (John 4:41). Or: "Unless you see signs and wonders you will not *believe*" (4:48). Or: "Whoever *believes* has eternal life" (6:47).

This absolute use of *believing*, with no object at all, suggests that John wants us to form an idea of the nature of *believing* that permeates all his uses. He expects us to fill up the meaning of *believing* from all its uses in his Gospel. I will argue that part of that meaning is the crucial affectional dimension we turn to now.

Believing Is Spiritual Drinking and Eating

The fact that Jesus spoke of himself as living water to be drunk (John 4:10–14; 6:35), and bread from heaven to be eaten (6:41, 48,

51), and the light of the world to be not just seen but loved (3:19) points to a kind of believing that is like eating the best food, and drinking the most satisfying water, and loving the most glorious light (cf. John 1:14).

In John 6:35–37, Jesus says:

> I am the bread of life; whoever *comes* to me shall not hunger, and whoever *believes* in me shall never thirst. But I said to you that you have seen me and yet do not *believe*. All that the Father gives me will *come* to me, and whoever comes to me I will never cast out.

The parallel in 6:35 between *coming* so as not to hunger and *believing* so as not to thirst tells us that Jesus saw this believing as coming, and this coming as believing. We see the parallel again in 6:36–37. Jesus observes in verse 36 that in spite of seeing him, some do not believe. Then in verse 37, he gives the underlying reason for this: "All [and *only* those] that the Father gives me will come to me." In other words, they did not believe because only those whom the Father has "given" to Jesus will "come." So not *coming* to Jesus in verse 37 is interchangeable with not *believing* in verse 36.

The very same sequence of thought comes out in John 6:64–65. Jesus says:

> "There are some of you who do not *believe*." (For Jesus knew from the beginning who those were who did not *believe*, and who it was who would betray him.) And he said, "This is why I told you that no one can *come* to me unless it is granted him by the Father."

In other words, the explanation for why some do not *believe* is that "no one can *come* to me unless it is granted him by the Father." The gift of *coming* is experienced as *believing*.

We will ask later how treating *believing* as *coming* (6:35) fits with treating believing as *receiving* (1:12). *Coming to* and *receiving from* seem like opposite movements of the soul. We will try to show how they fit together. But for now, the main thing I want us to see is the implication of the words *not hunger* and the words *never thirst* in verse 35:

| Whoever | comes to me | shall *not hunger* and |
| Whoever | believes in me | shall *never thirst* |

The words *not* and *never* imply that *coming* and *believing* issue in *eternal* life. John makes this explicit in 6:47 ("Whoever believes has eternal life") and 6:58 ("Whoever feeds on this bread will live forever").

Eternal Life Includes Eternal Life-Sharing

This eternal life is described as the experience of everlasting and complete satisfaction. Not hungering and never thirsting do not refer to *physical* drinking and eating. The woman at the well in chapter 4 had made this mistake when Jesus offered her to never thirst again: "Sir, you have nothing to draw water with, and the well is deep" (John 4:11). Jesus corrected her. I am not talking about physical water and physical thirst. I am not talking about the water in the well or the physical effects of it. I am talking about the deepest needs and longings of your soul.

Everyone who drinks of this water will be thirsty again, but whoever drinks of the water that I will give him will never be thirsty again. The water that I will give him will become in him a spring of water welling up to eternal life. (John 4:13–14)

So drinking the living water Christ offers leads not only to never-ending satisfaction ("never be thirsty again"), but also to the kind of satisfaction that overflows for others ("a spring of water welling up").

Jesus says this again in John 7:37–38. Again, he puts *believing in Jesus* and *coming to Jesus* together as parallel. And again, as in John 4:14, the effect of coming and believing is not only never to thirst, but to become a spring that gushes with eternal life:

On the last day of the feast, the great day, Jesus stood up and cried out, "If anyone thirsts, let him *come* to me and drink. Whoever *believes* in me, as the Scripture has said, 'Out of his heart will flow rivers of living water.'"

The reward of *coming* to Jesus, and *believing* in Jesus, and drinking the living water that he himself is—that reward is more than never thirsting again. It includes a life-giving overflow. Jesus knows that true satisfaction of soul comes to consummation with the kind of fullness that spills over for others. The gift of eternal life includes the gift of eternal life-sharing.

Believing Is Finding the Soul's Satisfaction in Jesus as Living Water

Circling back now to John 6:35, this is how I would describe believing: it is the heart's coming to Jesus so as to be forever satisfied in him. That is what the parallel shows.

| Whoever | *comes* to me | shall not hunger and |
| Whoever | *believes* in me | shall never thirst |

Believing is the heart's coming to Jesus in such a way that the soul finds the end of its quest for satisfaction. I use the word *satisfaction* because, even though Jesus said his aim was their *joy* (John 15:11; 17:13), we don't usually describe the effect of water and bread as joy. We say of a cold drink on a hot day, "That was satisfying." That is the analogy Jesus used. And if anything, the satisfaction of such a drink in the first century, when drinkable water was more precious, would have even been greater.

Loving the Light or Loving the Darkness: Believing or Not Believing

Jesus described believing not only as drinking water and eating bread, but also as loving light. In John 3:18–19, he said:

> Whoever *believes* in him is not condemned, but whoever does not *believe* is condemned already, because he has not *believed* in the name of the only Son of God. And this is the judgment: the light has come into the world, and people *loved the darkness* rather than the light because their works were evil.

There are two ways to describe the plight of the person who does not believe on Jesus. One is to describe it from God's side—that is, to say that he is under God's condemnation. He "is *condemned* already, because he has not *believed*" (3:18). The other is to describe the plight from the human side as the unbeliever's love of darkness: "This is the judgment: the light has come into the world, and people *loved the darkness* rather than the light" (3:19).

So, not believing in Christ as the light of the world (John 8:12) is described in 3:19 as *loving* "the darkness rather than the light." That is, not *believing* in the light is called not *loving* the light. The reason for unbelief is not the absence of light, but the love of darkness. It is an issue of what we *love* more deeply than an issue of what we *know*. This is exactly what we saw in 2 Thessalonians 2:10–12, where the failure to *love* the truth was virtually the same as the failure to *believe* in the truth (chapter 18). "They did not receive the *love* of the truth so as to be saved. . . . They did not *believe* the truth." So here in John 3—they do "not believe" because they "[love] the darkness."

As a Deer Pants for Flowing Streams

I conclude from Jesus's treatment of believing as we see it in John's Gospel that saving faith has an essential affectional dimension. That dimension is described as eating the bread of life so that our souls do not hunger (John 6:35, 51), and as drinking living water so as never to thirst again (John 4:10–11; 6:35; 7:38), and as loving the light of the world for the glorious brightness that he really is: "We have seen his glory, glory as of the only Son from the Father" (John 1:14; 3:19).

Surely we should not be surprised that Jesus would offer himself to the world as the fulfillment of the deepest longings expressed in the Psalms. This is the book he loved and in which he lived. This is the book that not only gave him the cry of forsakenness on the cross ("My God, my God, why have you forsaken me?" Matt. 27:46 = Ps. 22:1), but also gave him the assurance that those who believe in him would experience the kind of satisfaction that the human soul was created to enjoy. He said, "Whoever believes in me, *as the Scripture has said*, 'Out of his heart will flow rivers of living water'" (John 7:38).

No Scripture says that in just those words. He was speaking generally about what a life lived in the Scriptures had taught him. But how can we not think of the Psalms?

> In your presence there is fullness of joy;
>> at your right hand are pleasures forevermore. (Ps. 16:11)

> As a deer pants for flowing streams,
>> so pants my soul for you, O God.
> My soul thirsts for God,
>> for the living God. (Ps. 42:1–2)

> O God, you are my God; . . .
>> my soul thirsts for you;
> my flesh faints for you,
>> as in a dry and weary land where there is no water. . . .
> Your steadfast love is better than life. . . .
> My soul will be satisfied as with fat and rich food.
>> (Ps. 63:1, 3, 5)

> My flesh and my heart may fail,
>> but God is the strength of my heart and my portion
>> forever. (Ps. 73:26)

> He satisfies the longing soul. (Ps. 107:9)

> My soul thirsts for you like a parched land. (Ps. 143:6)

Surely, Jesus did not intend for us to come to him and find less than what the psalmists enjoyed in their fellowship with God. No.

Coming to Jesus—that is, believing on Jesus—was to see and savor the life-giving, soul-satisfying fulfillment of what the psalmists longed for, tasted, and enjoyed.

Coming to and Receiving From

I said above that I would deal with this question: How does believing as *coming to Jesus* (John 6:35) fit with believing as *receiving Jesus* (John 1:12)? One of the ways Jesus describes believing is coming to him so as to drink and never thirst again (John 6:35). But *coming to* and *receiving from* seem like opposite movements of the soul. How do they fit together? How is faith always essentially a *receiving of Christ* and yet also a *coming to Christ for the soul's eternal satisfaction?*

Part of the answer lies in realizing that *coming* is an act of the soul or the heart, not an act of the body. Just as eating the bread of heaven and drinking living water are not acts of the body, so coming to Christ as food and drink is not a physical movement. It is not done with muscles, but with the heart. It can be done as fully by a paralyzed person as by an athlete. So we must ask, How does the heart *come?*

No Space Traversed, No Time Elapsed

Just as there is no physical movement, neither is there any physical space to be traversed. The heart does not cross any geography. Not a mile. Not an inch. Not a millimeter. Therefore, there is no time to be crossed either. When the heart *comes* to Christ, it does not travel for an hour, or a minute, or a second, wondering if this coming will attain Christ.

The coming is the believing. And to the believing is given the promise of eternal life, instantly. "Whoever believes has eternal life" (John 6:47). There is no waiting—no time gap and no space gap between believing and life. To believe is to have eternal life. Therefore, to come is to have eternal life.

What kind of coming is this? How does the heart move? It moves with affections. It moves, for example, with hate, in repelling. It moves with love, in receiving. The coming of the heart to Christ savingly is the awakening in the heart of a preference for Christ over all others. It is not a grudging preference for one boring escape from hell over another. It is a happy preference because the Savior from hell is satisfying to the soul. He is water and bread and light. This preference is a desire. It is the soul's motion, with no space traversed or time elapsed.

When this gift of life and light happens, the soul is moving. It is coming to drink and eat. In the instant that living faith is created, the desiring heart turns from one fountain to another, one food to another, one treasure to another. This is the movement implied in the heart's *coming*.

Since there is no space for the soul to traverse in coming to Christ and no time to pass through, salvation (new birth, eternal life, justification) happens in the first twitch of God-given life—the first heartbeat of the soul's believing. In the very first instant of the miracle of finding our old treasure no longer compelling, but seeing Christ as our superior treasure—in that instant life and Christ are possessed, with all that God is for us in him.

The promise is, "Whoever comes to me I will never cast out" (John 6:37). The implication is that if we come to him, we are there. There is no "on the way" in the act of saving faith. There are many ways to be "on the way" to Christ. But in John's vocabulary, to "come to Christ" is to believe, and in believing to have eternal life instantly. The coming from which we will never be cast out is a saving coming. In the first instant of it, we are there. We are in Christ and he in us.

Whoever Has (Received) the Son Has Life

Now, with this clarification of "coming" to Christ, we are in a position to ponder the relationship between saving faith as *coming* to Christ and saving faith as *receiving* Christ. The term *receiving Christ*, by itself with no context, does not specify the disposition of the receiver. One can receive a person without liking him or without loving him or admiring or enjoying or trusting him. The word *receive* puts the focus on the fact that there is something or someone to be received. Receiving calls attention to the motion of the one being received. That person is moving toward the receiver—into relationship with the receiver. The emphasis falls on the need for the one being received.

This is absolutely crucial in describing the nature of saving faith. Nothing I have to say about the affectional nature of this receiving alters this truth. In saving faith, *another person* from outside ourselves moves toward us and into us. This is our only hope of salvation. We do not save ourselves. We must have a Savior from outside ourselves. Eternal life comes to us from outside ourselves. "Whoever has the Son has life" (1 John 5:12). When he is received in a saving way, he becomes ours. All that God is for us in him comes to us. It is received. *He* is received.

The Received Christ Remains Central as We Come and Drink

Such *receiving* is not the only way to describe saving faith. The description of faith as *receiving* does not exist in a vacuum. It is possible to *receive* in a way that does not save. "We appeal to you," Paul said, "not to *receive* the grace of God in vain" (2 Cor. 6:1).

Jesus describes the receiving that is not in vain. That's what we have seen in Jesus's words about eating him as food, and drinking him as water, and loving him as light. These pictures show us that the *receiving* that saves has an affectional dimension.

Therefore, to say that saving faith is the soul's *coming* to Jesus so as to be satisfied with all that God is for us in him does not contradict faith as *receiving*. It illuminates it. It defines receiving more fully. It brings out more of the dimensions of how saving faith is experienced in the human heart.

When I say that receiving Christ has an affectional dimension of coming to him for the soul's satisfaction, nothing alters the fact that *the received one* remains central. He remains central in our coming to him. The received Christ remains central as we put our lips to the cup of his life. The received Christ remains central as we bite down on the bread of heaven.[2]

The picture of *coming to Christ* adds to the picture of *receiving Christ*. What it adds is the movement of the soul toward Christ, in addition to the movement of Christ toward the soul. We have

---

2   Someone may object, "Faith receives. Christ satisfies. That is, drinking the cup of water was the act; the water itself satisfied. Faith is the act of receiving. The *result* is joy, satisfaction, etc., which are not *necessarily* part of the ontology of receiving." Or, as another objector might express it, "We first taste our meat, and then love it." My response is that there is a confusion of categories in the first objection. First, there is the category of the objective reality that satisfies, and then there is the category of the subjective experience of being satisfied. Therefore, we should not play them off against each other. The first reality (Christ, the treasure that satisfies) does not rule out the second (faith, the experience of being satisfied by Christ), but grounds it. Of course "faith receives and Christ satisfies." But my point—the point of this book—is that saving faith does *not* receive Christ as unsatisfyingly wet. It receives him as satisfying. Receiving Christ *as satisfying* (not just as a doctrine that he is satisfying) is an experience of satisfaction in Christ. This also is my answer to the second objection, "We first taste our meat, and then love it." The tasting is not a saving tasting unless it is "[tasting] that the Lord is good" (1 Pet. 2:3). There is no neutral act of tasting (believing) prior to the affectional act of treasuring (loving). One of the main points of this book is that tasting is a saving tasting only when it is a tasting as precious.

seen that the soul's movement is the awakening of desire for the received. That desire is a motion of the soul. It is the motion of God-given thirst putting its lips to the fountain of received water. It is the motion of God-given hunger placing its tongue on the richness of received bread. It is the motion of an embrace opening its arms to enclose the received Savior. It is the motion of leaning into the light of received glory. It is the motion of the glad and eager soul, opening the door for the friend (John 15:15) and helper (14:16) and Lord (13:14) and teacher (3:2).

Believe, the Insatiable Verb

I said I would venture a guess about why John uses the verb *believe* ninety-eight times in his Gospel and never uses the noun *belief* or *faith*. What you have just read is my guess. John loves to foreground the spiritual act of the soul in receiving and coming and drinking and eating and loving. He prefers to speak of believing this way rather than as a state or position of the soul. Believing is not so much a *condition* or a *state* as it is the *act* of the soul—a spiritual imbibing, ingesting, embracing, and savoring of the all-satisfying glories of Christ.

Believing is not even a *state* of satisfaction in Christ or a *state* of pleasure in Christ. Rather, John wants to emphasize that we never put down the cup of living water as though we've had enough. We never lay aside the loaf of heaven's bread as though we were stuffed. We never pull the curtain on the light of the world as though we'd seen enough glory for now. *Believing* doesn't do that.

Faith is receiving constantly and coming constantly. Christ is ever giving himself as drink and food and light for our souls. We are ever putting our lips to the cup and our tongue to the bread and our eyes to the light. Life in Christ is like a branch and a vine, not like a full cup sitting on a table beside a ready pitcher. "I am the vine; you are the branches. Whoever abides in me and I in him, he it is that bears much fruit, for apart from me you can do nothing" (John 15:5). Believing is what a branch does in the vine. It drinks. It eats. It never stops. It abides. To eternity.

There is doubtless more to be seen and said about why John loves the word *believe* more than the word *belief*. But oh how glad I am that he has given us words for the daily, everlasting experience of saving faith.

The Non-Surprise of Part 4

Again and again in parts 2 and 3 of this book, the affectional nature of saving faith intruded prematurely into our effort to describe faith generally (part 2) and to describe it as the reception of a treasure (part 3). The aim of part 4 has been to show that those intrusions were warranted.

If saving faith is like selling all, with joy, to receive the kingdom (Matt. 13:44),

if saving faith means loving Jesus more than our dearest relatives (Matt. 10:37),

if saving faith is designed to overcome anxiety (Matt. 8:26),

if saving faith is designed to overcome doubt (Matt. 14:31),

if saving faith embraces a promise to inherit the world (Rom. 4:13, 20),

if saving faith sees the very glory of God in Christ (2 Cor. 4:6),

if saving faith is the present realization of a hoped-for joy (Heb. 11:1; 12:2),

if saving faith knows Jesus as more valuable than all other privileges (Phil. 3:8), then should we be surprised that here in part 4 we have found that this faith is

- not just the receiving of Christ who is a treasure, but the treasuring of Christ (Heb. 11:25–26);
- not just agreeing that there is a joy set before us, but tasting now the substance of that joy (Heb. 11:1);
- not just knowing the truth of the gospel, but loving it and finding more pleasure in Christ than in unrighteousness (2 Thess. 2:10–12);
- not just affirming that our Father is more desirable than the desires of the flesh and the desires of the eyes, but actually loving him so as to overcome the world's distaste for God's commandments (1 John 5:3–4);
- not just discovering that Christ is the bread of life and the living water, but eating and drinking to the soul's satisfaction (John 6:35)?

No. We should not be surprised. For that is what we have found in God's word.

PART 5

CALLING FOR FAITH WHEN
FAITH IS AFFECTIONAL

Since I am finished with the exegetical heart of the book, it would seem fitting to offer a summary definition of saving faith. After all, the title of the book is *What Is Saving Faith?* I am willing to do that, but not because I can succeed. Every definition I have ever read from others or ventured to write myself is inadequate.

I have already said that "faith is such a living reality, responding to and reflecting rationally and affectionally such immeasurable glories of Christ, that to think of exhaustively defining or describing it is folly" (chap. 12n2). This is why I have written a book, not just an essay—let alone a sentence—defining saving faith. Every attempt at a definition (even those that are book-length) leave out important aspects of the real-life experience we call saving faith. Nevertheless, my definition follows below.

Summary Definition of Saving Faith

Saving faith is the God-given act of the human heart receiving, as its supreme treasure, Jesus Christ with all that God did for us and is for us in him.[1] You can see that the reason I am willing to venture such a definition is that my terms are so expansive that they are able to include vast and glorious realities that I do not mention.

- The word "receiving" encompasses the endless variations of the heart's believing, trusting, embracing, drinking, feeding, resting, expecting, hoping, being satisfied, delighting, enjoying, treasuring, etc.

- The words "as its supreme treasure" allow us to attach Christ's infinite worth to all his excellencies—treasured Lord, treasured Savior, treasured King, treasured wisdom, righteousness, redemption, helper, guide, friend, water, food, light, etc.

- The words "Jesus Christ" place him at the center as the one received and treasured supremely. He is the treasure and the sum of all good.

- The words "with all that God did for us and is for us in him" offer the most glorious and frustrating generalization. It includes all that Christ accomplished in his life, on the cross, in the resurrection, and in his ascension; all that Christ is accomplishing now in his heavenly intercession; and all that

---

1   I'm not limiting "heart" here to the organ of spiritual affections only, but including also the heart's biblical function as giving rise to thoughts (Matt. 15:19).

Christ will accomplish in his second coming and eternal reign. It includes not only all that God *did* in Christ, but all that God *is* for us in him—and that is as vast and as satisfying as the being of God himself.

- The words "in him" secure the eternally unbreakable unity between what God the Father is and does for us, and what God the Son is and does for us. There is no benefit from the Son nor pleasure in the Son that is not also a benefit from the Father and a pleasure in the Father.

Should we feel dismay that such vastness of meaning for saving faith puts it beyond what a child can experience, or beyond what a person with little awareness of the biblical story can experience? No! And the reason is that in every conversion to Christian faith (from the simplest child to the PhD), the scope of knowledge and the intensity of response are limited and varied. The convert needs enough of the gospel so that the Holy Spirit, through it, can grant an authentic sight of Christ and his saving work, and thus awaken saving faith. That faith receives and treasures Christ in whatever measure of truth has been shared. The authenticity of that infant faith will be proven by the happy welcome of every new vista of Christ's truth and beauty.

Six Implications

What remains then for me to do within the bounds of this book is to spell out six implications of what we have seen (part 5), and, finally, to relate our findings to the glory of God and his ultimate purposes in creation (conclusion). The implications relate to six questions:

1. If saving faith is an affectional embrace of Christ as our supreme treasure, how then in our evangelism do we call for such faith? How do we lead people into this experience?

2. Specifically, what becomes of Christ's demand that people "count the cost" of discipleship before they follow him (Luke 14:28)? Does that fit with faith as the awakening of the spiritual affection of treasuring Christ?

3. What about the biblical pattern of warning unbelievers of impending judgment? How will such warnings lead to the awakening of a "warm embrace" of Christ?

4. What is repentance and how does it relate to receiving Christ as a treasure? Is repentance necessary for a saving conversion to Christ?

5. Have you made conversion essentially impossible? In our evangelism, it seems hopeful that we can call for a *decision*. But it does not seem hopeful to try to create a spiritual *affection*.

6. Finally, in the fight of faith, have you undermined the precious experience of assurance? The affections are so variable, going up and down, how will we ever enjoy the assurance that we belong to Christ?

To these we now turn, addressing one question in each remaining chapter.

21

The Offer of Treasure

ONE OF MY EARNEST PRAYERS for this book is that God would use it to make us more fruitful in calling others to saving faith in Christ. I have tried to clarify from Scripture what we are calling people to in our evangelism. What, then, are the implications of this book for leading others to Christ, whether personally in conversation at a coffee shop or when preaching in worship or in the open air?

Tell of His Excellencies

Paul tells Timothy, and thus all pastors and elders, "Do the work of an evangelist" (2 Tim. 4:5). And Peter broadens out the mandate to all Christians: "You are a chosen race, a royal priesthood, a holy nation, a people for his own possession, *that you may proclaim the excellencies of him* who called you out of darkness into his marvelous light" (1 Pet. 2:9). Three verses later, he says that the aim of this proclamation is that the excellencies of Christ, adorned with good deeds, would lead others to "glorify God on the day of visitation" (1 Pet. 2:12).

The words *evangelist* and *evangelism* come from the word *evangel*, which is the English form of the Greek word εὐαγγέλιον (*euaggelion*), which means "gospel" or "good news." To evangelize is to proclaim the good news. We proclaim the good news to unbelievers, calling them to faith in Christ. And we proclaim the good news to believers, calling them into greater depths of gospel understanding and believing and living. When Peter said that the task of believers is to "proclaim the excellencies of him who called you out of darkness," he was describing evangelism because the good news is most essentially the offer of Christ in the fullness of the excellencies of his person and the perfection of his achievements.

Christ, the Greatest Good of the Gospel

We can see this if we trace the proclamation of the gospel up to its apex in the glory of Christ. Paul repeatedly calls the gospel the "gospel of Christ" (Rom. 15:19; 2 Cor. 9:13; 10:14; Gal. 1:7; Phil. 1:27; 1 Thess. 3:2). It is the gospel that Christ brought and that he preached. It is the gospel of which he himself is the highest gift and treasure.

When Paul described his preaching of the gospel, he could simply say, "We preach *Christ*" (1 Cor. 1:23). Or when describing his calling to preach the gospel, he could say, "To me . . . this grace was given, to preach to the Gentiles *the unsearchable riches of Christ*" (Eph. 3:8). And when he described the content of the gospel that Satan hides from unbelievers, he could call it "the light of *the gospel of the glory of Christ*, who is the image of God" (2 Cor. 4:4). "The glory of Christ" is the greatest good of the good news—the glory of Christ seen and savored and shared. "To this he called you through our gospel, so that you may *obtain the glory of our Lord Jesus Christ*" (2 Thess. 2:14). The greatest gift of the gospel of Christ is Christ, and all that God is for us in him.

Achievements and Riches of Christ

Of course, no sinner can expect to have Christ while his sins are unforgiven. We must be saved from our sins (Matt. 1:21). So the gospel is called "the gospel of your salvation" (Eph. 1:13). The unsearchable riches of Christ include "redemption through his blood, the forgiveness of our trespasses, according to the riches of his grace" (Eph. 1:7). And those riches of grace also include the gift of eternal life and joy. Thus, God makes his people alive in Christ Jesus "so that in the coming ages he might show the immeasurable riches of his grace in kindness toward us in Christ Jesus" (Eph. 2:7). All that Christ is and does to achieve our salvation, climaxing in the eternal enjoyment of his unsearchable riches, is included in the good news of Christ.[1]

So when we evangelize—that is, when we proclaim (or share with a neighbor) the gospel—we most essentially and most ultimately offer *Christ* to people—Christ himself. To be sure, with great joy, we offer forgiveness of sins (Acts 10:43), justification in the court of heaven (Rom. 8:30), peace with God and freedom from his wrath (Rom. 5:1; 1 Thess. 1:10), triumph over the fear of death (Heb. 2:14), resurrection with a new and glorious body (Phil. 3:21), eternal life (John 3:16), the indwelling and sealing of the Holy Spirit (Rom. 8:11; Eph. 1:13), fellowship with the Son of God (1 Cor. 1:9), the greatest purpose to live for (2 Cor. 5:15), unfailing hope (Col. 1:5), and inexpressible joy (1 Peter 1:8). The "riches of Christ" are inexhaustible. In our evangelism, we can't mention them all each time we share the gospel. So we pray for discernment to know which of the

---

1 For a fuller explanation and support for God himself in Christ as the highest and best gift of the gospel, see John Piper, *God Is the Gospel: Meditations on God's Love as the Gift of Himself* (Wheaton, IL: Crossway, 2005).

countless gifts of the gospel to bring out of the treasure chest of Christ's riches.

Evangelism Offers Christ and All in Him

In all our effort to display the gifts of the good news, the indispensable thing to offer is Christ. In Christ are hidden all the treasures. If we have Christ, we have all that he is for us and all that he achieved for us. If the person we are evangelizing receives Christ, he will spend eternity joyfully discovering the fullness of what he has received in Christ.

John Murray (1898–1975), longtime professor of theology at Westminster Seminary, described the work of evangelism and the free offer of the gospel this way:

> It is Christ who is offered. More strictly *he* offers himself. The whole gamut of redemptive grace is included. Salvation in all of its aspects and in the furthest reaches of glory consummated is the overture. For Christ is the embodiment of all. Those who are his are complete in him and he is made unto them wisdom from God, and righteousness, and sanctification, and redemption. When Christ invites us to himself it is to the possession of himself and therefore of all that defines his identity as Lord and Saviour.[2]

Christ is the one offered in the gospel. All other blessings are in him. If we receive him, we have them. He is offered freely to all.

---

2   John Murray, "The Atonement and Free Offer of the Gospel," in *Collected Writings of John Murray*, vol. 1, *The Claims of Truth* (Carlisle, PA: Banner of Truth, 1976), 82; emphasis original. In what follows, I have adapted several paragraphs from my chapter "'My Glory I Will Not Give to Another,' Preaching the Fullness of Definite Atonement to the Glory of God," in *From Heaven He Came and Sought Her: Definite Atonement in Historical, Theological, and Pastoral Perspective*, ed. David Gibson and Jonathan Gibson (Wheaton, IL: Crossway, 2013), 633–67.

He gives himself to all who come. He is offered freely, and he never denies himself to any who meet the terms of the offer.

Whoever!

What are these terms? Believe Christ. Receive Christ.

To all who did receive him, who believed in his name, he gave the right to become children of God. (John 1:12)

Whoever believes in him is not condemned. (John 3:18)

Whoever believes in the Son has eternal life. (John 3:36; 6:47)

Whoever comes to me I will never cast out. (John 6:37)

Whoever comes to me shall not hunger, and whoever believes in me shall never thirst. (John 6:35)

Whoever receives me receives the one who sent me. (John 13:20; see also Matt. 10:40)

Whoever believes in me, though he die, yet shall he live. (John 11:25)

Believe in the Lord Jesus, and you will be saved. (Acts 16:31)

In our evangelism, we take seriously all these expansive *whoevers*. We offer Christ in all his personal glory and with all his saving benefits to everyone and anyone who will believe. We make no distinctions. We do not try to discern who the elect are. We do not look for evidences of God's calling. We do not play favorites with race or ethnicity or class or sex or educational levels or wealth or degrees of sinfulness.

We indiscriminately proclaim to everyone, "Receive Christ, and your sins will be covered. Receive Christ, and your condemnation will be removed." We entreat and implore. We say with Paul, "We are ambassadors for Christ, God making his appeal through us. We implore you on behalf of Christ, be reconciled to God" (2 Cor. 5:20). We plead, if possible with tears: "Come! 'Take the water of life without price'" (Rev. 22:17). He will not reject you. All that he is, and all that he achieved in dying and rising and reigning, will be yours."

Every Convert Receives More Than He Knows

Although new converts to Christ do not need to know—indeed cannot know all at once—the fullness of God's complete achievement of their everlasting salvation, nevertheless, that is what we offer in evangelism. We offer all the benefits that Christ's death secured for his people. They were chosen before the foundation of the world (Eph. 1:4). They were predestined for adoption (Eph. 1:5). Their new birth and faith and justification and sanctification and preservation and glorification were decisively purchased and secured by the blood of the new covenant (Luke 22:20). When Christ cried, "It is finished" (John 19:30), that covenant was sealed and sure for God's elect forever.

The bride is purchased (Eph. 5:25). Her coming and believing and obeying and persevering and eternal glory are as sure as the faithfulness of God and the value of his Son's blood. Every blessing in the heavenly places is guaranteed (Eph. 1:3)—all the promises of God (2 Cor. 1:20), all things working together for their good

(Rom. 8:28), no good thing withheld (Ps. 84:11), and in the end, sinless and all-satisfying fellowship with God forever (1 Pet. 3:18). All this is offered in evangelism. Because all of it is in Christ. And Christ is the sum of what we offer in proclaiming the gospel. This is what he achieved in his life and death and resurrection. To have him is to have it all.

Compassionate and Confident World Missions

It should be obvious, but I will make it explicit: this vision of evangelism and the free offer of the gospel for whoever will receive it propels us into the great work of world missions with compassion and confidence: *compassion*, because we have been so loved ourselves and because God has put within us a longing for others to join us in this great salvation; *confidence*, because contained in the atonement itself is the power of the gospel to raise the spiritually dead and bring people to faith, however deep their opposition.

We are carried in our passion for the unreached peoples of the world by the spectacular person of Christ and the stupendous achievement of his cross. We do not hesitate to say to every person in every people group that God loves you and offers you in Christ the fullest possible redemption in everlasting, all-satisfying fellowship with himself (John 3:16). This message is valid and this offer is sincere to every person on the planet. And it is breathtakingly glorious. How could we not want to bring this news to every person and every people group in the world?

What about the Treasure?

Someone may ask at this point, "Why have you not used the words 'as a treasure' in your gospel presentation? You have repeatedly referred to believing Christ and receiving Christ but have not once said, 'Believe him as your treasure,' or 'Receive him as your treasure.' Why not?"

For two reasons.

Not Just Saying Words, but Seeing Reality

First, the aim of this book is not mainly to change the words we use in evangelism. The aim is to change the way we see reality. Appropriate words will follow. And they may be different in every gospel presentation.

The reality I am trying to make plain is that Christ is the central and greatest good of the good news. He is the sum of all good—all the good that he *is* as supremely great and glorious and valuable, and all the good that he *secured* in his death and resurrection. And he himself, therefore, is infinitely precious, desirable, and satisfying. *He himself* is the supreme treasure of the universe and of the gospel.

Saving faith—saving believing and receiving—means believing and receiving him for who he is. Saving faith does not see Christ as useful to obtain something treasured more than Christ. Saving faith sees Christ for who he is: all-glorious (2 Cor. 4:4) and therefore all-satisfying (John 6:35). Saving faith, therefore, embraces Christ as its supreme treasure in all the inexpressibly valuable gifts of the gospel.

That is the *reality* I am trying to make plain in this book. *How that gets expressed* in countless gospel presentations among millions of individuals and thousands of unreached peoples with varied cultures and languages, I do not presume to prescribe. Language matters. But reality matters more. And for people of integrity, reality governs language choices. Those who see the reality and love it and long to see others embrace it will labor prayerfully and biblically to find true and helpful words in every evangelistic situation.

Tasting Sweetness Is Better than Saying It's Sweet

The second reason I have not *insisted* on using the phrase "receive Christ *as your treasure*" is that the goal of evangelism is not for people to adopt a new phrase to describe their faith; the goal is for people to *experience a miracle* called the new birth. In that miracle, their hearts will actually taste the beauty and worth and desirability of Christ. This taste is infinitely more important than being able to put words on it.

It is more important that people taste honey as sweet than that they learn the sentence "Honey is sweet." They may never hear that sentence and yet enjoy the sweetness of honey more than those who know the sentence, "Honey is sweet," but cannot taste it. A person's heart may be totally redeemed and renovated by receiving Christ as supremely valuable and satisfying, and yet never in their lives hear or speak this sentence: "Saving faith is receiving Christ as a supreme treasure."

Telling people that honey is sweet *might* help them taste and experience the sweetness. And telling people that Christ is a treasure *might* help them experience Christ as a treasure. But natural emotions and spiritual affections don't usually work that way. Telling me to enjoy a food that I don't like does not usually cause me to like it. Telling an unbeliever *that* Christ is a great and satisfying treasure does not usually create a treasuring of Christ. This is why, in my effort to describe how we proclaim the gospel, I tried to describe some of the particulars of *how* Christ is great and what his achievements actually are.

It is good to tell people that honey is sweet and that Christ is a treasure. It is better to offer people a taste of honey and to tell them some precious particulars of Christ's glory and some spectacular specifics about what he offers in the gospel. Don't mistake what I'm saying. I think using the actual language of the affections, like "treasuring Christ" and "cherishing Christ" and "being satisfied in Christ," can be very helpful to awaken people to the fact that they may be missing the real thing. But what I am stressing here is that the reality of *experiencing Christ as a treasure* is not necessarily awakened by telling someone that Christ is a treasure, but is more often awakened when we get specific and actually describe Christ's beauty and greatness and value, especially if people can also see our own authentic satisfaction in him.[3]

Christ Is Always Shown as the Treasure

All our evangelism, in content and demeanor, should aim to show Christ as supremely valuable. In our evangelism, Christ will *always* be presented as the supreme treasure. Sometimes we will use those words. *Saying* to people, "Treasure Christ!" is sometimes useful. *Showing* him to be a treasure is always useful. Words matter a lot. Reality matters most.

Whatever aspect of his person we highlight, or whatever gift of the gospel we offer, we should do it with biblically saturated language that calls attention to Christ himself as the greatest treasure. If we speak of the sweetness of *forgiveness*, let it be plain that what makes it sweet is not mainly a clean conscience, and not mainly escape from hell (as inestimable as those are!), but mainly guilt-free fellowship with Jesus (1 Cor. 1:9), and access to the enjoyment of God himself (1 Pet. 3:18). If we speak of *eternal life and the*

---

3 I felt this burden of sharing specific glories of Christ so keenly some years ago that I wrote a short book called *Seeing and Savoring Jesus Christ* (Wheaton, IL: Crossway, 2001). The conviction behind it was what I am saying here: if people are to be awakened to Christ as a supreme treasure, they need to hear not just *that* he is, but *how* he is.

resurrection body free from pain, let it be plain that our new body will be precious mainly because it will be fitted to see and enjoy the glories of God without being incinerated, and that it will be pain-free lest we be distracted in taking in the eternal pleasures at God's right hand (Ps. 16:11).

New Birth, Not Just New Language

Those are my two reasons for describing how we do evangelism without insisting that we always use the central language of this book—namely, that saving faith is a receiving of Christ as our supreme treasure, or that saving faith is treasuring and enjoying and being satisfied in all that God is for us in Christ. My aim is not primarily that more and more people use *treasuring* language, but that more and more people *actually treasure* Christ as supreme. I think the language is helpful. I think it will follow in its proper place. But it's not the goal. The goal is real Christians instead of nominal ones. The goal is new birth, not just new language. The goal is hearts that treasure Christ, not just mouths that speak it.

22

Counting the Cost of
Embracing the Treasure

EVEN THOUGH I THINK our evangelism should be dominated by the display of the "unsearchable riches of Christ" (since showing treasures is the best way to stir up treasuring), that does not rule out (1) the call to count the cost, (2) the use of warnings, and (3) the command to repent. Jesus and the apostles used all three of these in their preaching and in their effort to bring forth saving faith. So I am asking, How does the point of this book relate to these three strategies in evangelism? The next three chapters take them up one at a time.

Paul's Candor about the Cost of Following Christ

It appears that Paul, in his evangelistic preaching, not only magnified the "unsearchable riches of Christ," but also made clear that receiving Christ will bring tribulations. In other words, he wanted people to count the cost of following Christ. We know he said this kind of thing to new believers. When Paul and Barnabas returned to strengthen the young churches they had recently planted, Luke tells us, they "returned . . . strengthening the souls of the disciples, encouraging them to continue in the faith, and saying that *through many tribulations we must enter the kingdom of God*" (Acts 14:21–22). Similarly, Paul said to Timothy, "Indeed, all who desire to live a godly life in Christ Jesus will be persecuted" (2 Tim. 3:12).

But there is good reason to think that Paul made this kind of message part of his initial evangelism as well. When he wrote to the brand-new church in Thessalonica, he said he had sent Timothy back to them "to establish and exhort you in your faith, that no one be moved by these afflictions. *For you yourselves know that we are destined for this*" (1 Thess. 3:2–3). In other words, he had already told them in the earliest days what to expect. There is no reason to think that Paul would try to lure people to Christ by hiding the cost of being a Christian, since he made it prominent and plain to the newest of believers.

Jesus: No Bait and Switch

Paul's pattern of encouraging converts to count the cost is not surprising in view of the way Jesus put the cost right up front in his evangelism. The most striking text is Luke 14:25–33:

> Now great crowds accompanied him, and he turned and said to them, "If anyone comes to me and does not hate his own father and mother and wife and children and brothers and sisters, yes, and even his own life, he cannot be my disciple. Whoever does not bear his own cross and come after me cannot be my disciple. For which of you, desiring to build a tower, does not first sit down and count the cost, whether he has enough to complete it? Otherwise, when he has laid a foundation and is not able

to finish, all who see it begin to mock him, saying, 'This man began to build and was not able to finish.' Or what king, going out to encounter another king in war, will not sit down first and deliberate whether he is able with ten thousand to meet him who comes against him with twenty thousand? And if not, while the other is yet a great way off, he sends a delegation and asks for terms of peace. So therefore, any one of you who does not renounce all that he has cannot be my disciple."

Jesus states the fourfold cost of coming to him so as to be his disciple: (1) hating all our family members (v. 26), (2) hating our own lives (v. 26), (3) bearing our own cross (v. 27), and (4) renouncing all we have (v. 33).

Two Clues on Counting the Cost

Two clues help me see what is really at stake here. First, it is odd that after illustrating the cost of discipleship with a builder that might not have enough money to finish his tower, and a king that might not have enough soldiers to win a battle, Jesus draws this conclusion: you can't be my disciple unless you renounce all you have (Luke 14:33). It's odd because the illustrations ask, "Do you have enough?" and the conclusion says, "Get rid of what you have." That's a clue.

Here's the other clue. Right after saying that we must hate our own lives in order to be his disciple, Jesus adds that we must bear our own cross (14:27). So he describes in two ways how we must deal with ourselves in coming to Christ. One is hate. The other is to be willing to suffer and die. I take the second to clarify the first. In other words, the emotion of hate toward oneself accomplishes little, especially if it carries the ordinary connotation of feeling hostility. Feeling angry and hostile toward myself does not serve Jesus. So Jesus clarifies: "What I mean by *hate* is that you will be willing to endure things for me (as my disciple) that will look like self-hate, because the world will simply think you are throwing your life away for a myth."

So both clues point in the same direction. Counting the cost does *not* mean, Do you have enough in this world to be my disciple? Instead, it means, Are you willing to lose the valuable things you have, even if it looks like hate? Following Christ has often meant that the disciple loses family members. To choose Christ at the cost of losing family will look as if you hate your family. To choose prison or execution over denying Christ will look as if you hate your life.

Do You Have Enough Treasure in Me?

If the only way to become a follower of Jesus, a true disciple, is by *saving faith*, as Jesus says it is (John 3:36; 11:25–26), what does this text about counting the cost tell us about the nature of saving faith? First, it tells us that some of the inner dynamics of saving faith are being described here. Jesus is not contradicting himself as though there were two ways of salvation. We become Jesus's true disciples—not Judas-like disciples, but John-like—by saving faith. We become the kind of disciples whom Jesus keeps forever (Luke 22:32; John 10:27–28) by receiving him as the supreme treasure of our lives. That is what saving faith does. And that is what this text is about.

When Jesus asks if the tower-builder has "enough" to finish (Luke 14:28) and if the king has "enough" to win (14:31), he is pointing to something positive. Do you have enough? Enough what? He ends the illustrations like this: "You have to renounce all you have." That is, you have to want me more than you want your possessions.

That's the issue. This is not a random story about self-sacrifice. This is a story about what it involves to follow Jesus and be saved. And the bottom line of the story is this: Jesus is worth more than family, possessions, and earthly life.

The question "Do you have enough?" comes down to this: "*Do you have enough treasure in me to move you to let other treasures go?* If you have not yet found your supreme treasure in me, you are not ready to be my disciple."

Reversal of What We Treasure

In another text, Jesus confirms that this is the point. He describes family loss and cross-bearing as loving him more than family. The issue, now, is not "hate" of family, but greater love for Jesus:

> I have come to set a man against his father, and a daughter against her mother, and a daughter-in-law against her mother-in-law. And a person's enemies will be those of his own household. Whoever loves father or mother more than me is not worthy of me, and whoever loves son or daughter more than me is not worthy of me. And whoever does not take his cross and follow me is not worthy of me. (Matt. 10:35–38)

I argued in chapter 14 that the love referred to here is the kind of love we have for those most precious to us. And I argued that being "worthy" of Jesus does not mean to be deserving of his salvation but rather to be a suitable object of his saving acceptance. In other words, this text describes the way we come into a saving relationship with Jesus. We come by experiencing a change in our hearts. And that change is that we treasure Jesus more than family or earthly life.

Count the Cost, Measure the Treasure

So in our evangelism, there is a place for urging people to count the cost. And the cost they are to count is this: As you consider your great need of a Savior and your great longing for eternal happiness, and as you consider the greatness and the glory and the worth of Jesus as the Son of God, and as you consider the all-sufficiency of his death for the forgiveness of sins and his resurrection for eternal joy, do you find in your heart that Jesus is more needful and more precious to you than all earthly treasure? Are you ready to receive him and believe in him as your supreme treasure, even if it costs you the loss of your family and your life?

Counseling people to count the cost means calling for a true estimate of the worth of Christ.

23

Warning People to Flee
from Judgment to Joy

THE FOCUS OF THE PREVIOUS chapter was the cost of having saving faith. The focus of this chapter is the cost of *not* having saving faith. Both are significant in New Testament evangelism.

Warnings of Jesus and Paul

No one in the Bible warned people about the danger of being *thrown* into hell more often than Jesus.[1] In some circles today, Jesus is portrayed as the tender, forgiving, party-going friend of sinners, while Paul is portrayed as the dour, cold, pitiless inventor of puritanical Christianity. It's a lopsided portrayal for both. Jesus warns explicitly about hell eleven times, while Paul never uses the

---

1 Some teachers today put the emphasis on people *choosing* hell by refusing the grace of God in general and special revelation. There is a sense in which that is true. It is not the way Jesus spoke. He spoke of God *throwing* people there, not of any voluntary leap. For more reflections on choosing hell versus "being thrown" there, see my article "How Willingly Do People Go to Hell?," October 28, 2009, Desiring God website, https://www.desiring god.org/.

word. And Jesus refers to it as a place of "eternal fire" (Matt. 18:8), and "outer darkness" (Matt. 8:12), and "weeping and gnashing of teeth" (Luke 13:28), and "torment" (Luke 16:23).

Paul may not use the word *hell* (γέεννα, *gehenna*), but he warns about the reality—namely, "the punishment of eternal destruction, away from the presence of the Lord and from the glory of his might" (2 Thess. 1:9). He warns the unbelieving hypocrite:

> Do you suppose, O man—you who judge those who practice such things and yet do them yourself—that you will escape the judgment of God? Or do you presume on the riches of his kindness and for-bearance and patience, not knowing that God's kindness is meant to lead you to repentance? But because of your hard and impenitent heart you are storing up wrath for yourself on the day of wrath when God's righteous judgment will be revealed. (Rom. 2:3–5)

When Paul labored with tears and pleadings to win his Jewish kinsmen to faith in Jesus as the Messiah (Rom. 9:2–3; 10:1; Phil. 3:18) but found them resistant, he said, "It was necessary that the word of God be spoken first to you. Since you thrust it aside and judge yourselves unworthy of eternal life, behold, we are turning to the Gentiles" (Acts 13:45–46). This was a warning: if you reject Jesus, you reject life. For "whoever has the Son has life; whoever does not have the Son of God does not have life" (1 John 5:12). The warnings of impending judgment are even called part of Paul's *gospel*. "According to my gospel, God judges the secrets of men by Christ Jesus" (Rom. 2:16).

Warnings in the Service of Love

The question I am raising about our evangelism is, How do warnings of judgment relate to the nature of saving faith as treasuring

Christ above all? The question is all the more urgent because many people think and feel that such warnings can serve only fear, not love. After all, didn't John write, "There is no fear in love, but perfect love casts out fear. For fear has to do with punishment, and whoever fears has not been perfected in love" (1 John 4:18)? So how can threats of punishment serve love?

Paul clearly believed that such warnings of punishment could indeed serve love, not just fear. For example, he said, "If anyone has no love for the Lord, let him be accursed" (1 Cor. 16:22). Remember, Paul was ready to be cursed himself, if it were possible, for the sake of winning people to Christ (Rom. 9:2). He poured out his life on the sacrificial offering of the faith of his converts (Phil. 2:17). Therefore, he spoke from this longing, and under the inspiration of God, when he said, "If you don't love him, you perish!"

Of course, we all know, and Paul knows, that when you shout to a person who is about to eat a poisonous mushroom, "Don't eat that! It will kill you!" that shout does not make him love good mushrooms. But it is a shout of love. And it does keep him alive so that by some means he may come to enjoy eating good mushrooms. In other words, warnings of judgment do not immediately endear the hearts of the warned to God. Christ does not appear beautiful just because hell appears hot.

Driven from a Burning House to the Daylight of Beauty

We know that no one gets into heaven simply because he has been scared out of hell. But how many little children, or even teenagers, have been held back from soul-destroying sin by the fear of hell just long enough for them to wake up to the beauties of heaven and the glory of Christ? When Paul said, "If anyone has no love for the Lord, let him be accursed," he did not expect that hypocrites in the church would immediately say, "Oh, how beautiful and wonderful and desirable is the Christ who will curse me for not loving him!" In fact, we can almost be certain that some would say cynically, "You expect me to love such a Lord!"

I think Paul's response to that would be, "I do not expect you to love a God who gives only threatenings and punishment. I have spoken my warning at the end of my letter in the hopes that it will send you back to what I have written. I have shown you that this very Lord who warns from heaven 'died for our sins' (1 Cor 15:3). I have tried to entice you to the banquet of Christ's love not with fear but with unimagined pleasures. 'What no eye has seen, nor ear heard, nor the heart of man imagined, . . . God has prepared for those who love him' (1 Cor. 2:9). You can mock my warning, if you will. But my gospel and my life are meant to lure you into joy with unimaginable treasures that God has prepared for those who love him. Don't spurn this. If you cannot yet taste it as a treasure, as satisfying to your soul, at least be reluctant to push it away. Keep looking, keep praying. God may yet open your eyes. My prayer is that my warning will drive you from the burning house of sin into the daylight of Christ's beauty."

Terror Serves Treasuring

Paul did not consider the warnings of judgment, or the fearful flight from it, as an obstacle to saving faith. Not when used in love. He warned believing Gentiles who were tempted to boast over unbelieving Jews, "They [the unbelieving Jews] were broken off because of their unbelief, but you stand fast through faith. So do not become proud, but *fear*. For if God did not spare the natural branches, neither will he spare you" (Rom. 11:20–21).

In other words, if pride gains the ascendency in your life and leads you to make shipwreck of your faith so that your so-called faith proves to be "in vain" (1 Cor. 15:2), you will be broken off like a branch and thrown into the fire (John 15:6). Why did Paul say this? He said it so that *they would stand fast in their faith.* "They were broken off because of their *unbelief,* but you stand fast through *faith.*" Could he have made it clearer that the fear of judgment has a place in serving faith? The terrors of hell serve the treasuring of Christ.

Great Gift of Being Warned

When I find in my heart a spirit of pride or lust or covetousness starting to rise, the prospect of these sins gaining ground in my life and blinding me to the all-satisfying beauties of Christ terrifies me. This is exactly what Paul said it should do. "Do not become proud, but *fear.* Do not become lustful, but *fear.* Do not become covetous, but *fear.*" Oh how thankful I am that the merciful Spirit of God has awakened this fear in me whenever it was needed to drive me out of the creeping blindness of suicidal sin into the brightness of the beauty of Christ.

Beware, Christian. Many have been taught unbiblical things about the place of warnings and the fear of God in our evangelism and in our own perseverance. If your view of justification by faith and the security of God's elect causes you to think that you are beyond the need to fear God's judgment and warn people of it, you do not yet know as you ought to know. Warnings are a means of grace in evangelism and in the perseverance of God's elect. Warnings do not make us love Christ. But they may hold us back from the darkness where his worth will never be seen again. Oh, how great the gift, how great the grace, that we are warned.

24

Repentance, the Renovation
of the Heart's Desire

WE HAVE SEEN THAT in our evangelism the call to treasure Christ is served by warnings about the cost of believing and the cost of not believing. Now we ask, What does it mean that "[God] commands all people everywhere to repent" (Acts 17:30)? And how does this command relate to the command to believe and to treasure Christ above all? And how does it shape our evangelism?[1]

Repentance: Basic to the Message of the New Testament

The command to repent is foundational to the message of Jesus. We will see that it is almost synonymous with the command, "You must be born again" (John 3:7). When he began his public ministry, the first command Jesus spoke was "Repent." "From that time Jesus began to preach, saying, 'Repent, for the kingdom of heaven

---

1 Some of what follows in this section is adapted from my article "Thoughts on Jesus's Demand to Repent: Letters from Cambridge #2," April 19, 2006, Desiring God website, https://www.desiringgod.org/.

is at hand'" (Matt. 4:17; cf. Mark 1:15). He said that the call to repentance was the very reason he had come into the world: "I have not come to call the righteous but sinners to repentance" (Luke 5:32). The requirement of repentance in his presence is connected to the unique greatness of who he was: "The men of Nineveh will rise up at the judgment with this generation and condemn it, for they repented at the preaching of Jonah, and behold, *something greater than Jonah is here*" (Matt. 12:41).

The command to repent remained basic to the evangelistic message of the apostles. Peter began his public ministry on Pentecost with the command "*Repent* therefore, and turn back, that your sins may be blotted out" (Acts 3:19). Paul brought his message in Athens to a climax when he said, "The times of ignorance God overlooked, but now he commands all people everywhere to *repent*" (Acts 17:30).

Twice Paul summed up his message with the command to repent. Saying farewell to the Ephesian elders, he said, "I did not shrink from declaring to you anything that was profitable . . . testifying both to Jews and to Greeks of *repentance* toward God and of faith in our Lord Jesus Christ" (Acts 20:20–21). When he was on trial near the end of his life, he said to King Agrippa, "I was not disobedient to the heavenly vision, but declared first to those in Damascus, then in Jerusalem and throughout all the region of Judea, and also to the Gentiles, that they should *repent* and turn to God, performing deeds in keeping with their repentance" (Acts 26:19–20).

Repentance, the Doorway to Eternal Life

What was at stake in this pervasive command of Jesus and the apostles? Why was it so common and so urgent? What hung in the balance was forgiveness of sins, escape from divine judgment, and the attainment of eternal life. Jesus said, as he commissioned his apostles for their worldwide mission, "Thus it is written, that the Christ should suffer and on the third day rise from the dead, and that *repentance for the forgiveness of sins* should be proclaimed in his name to all nations, beginning from Jerusalem" (Luke 24:46–47). The connection between repentance and forgiveness is implicit in Acts 5:31, where Peter says, "God exalted [Jesus] at his right hand as Leader and Savior, to give *repentance to Israel and forgiveness of sins.*" And the connection becomes explicit again as Peter connects repentance and forgiveness in warning Simon the magician about his "wickedness": "*Repent,* therefore, of this wickedness of yours, and pray to the Lord that, if possible, the intent of your heart may be *forgiven* you" (Acts 8:22).

The reason forgiveness of sins is so crucial is that without forgiveness of sins people perish. Jesus makes the connection between repentance and the escaping of God's judgment explicit in Luke 13:3: "Unless you repent, you will all likewise perish" (Luke 13:3). John the Baptist had made the connection even more explicit: "You brood of vipers! Who warned you to flee from the wrath to come? Bear fruits in keeping with repentance. And do not begin to say to yourselves, 'We have Abraham as our father'" (Luke 3:7–8). Without repentance there is no escape from the wrath of God. Or to put it positively, through repentance one will have eternal life. This is what the church concluded when they realized that the Gentiles had received the gift of the Holy Spirit: "Then to the Gentiles also God has granted repentance *that leads to life*" (Acts 11:18).

A Problem That Does Not Need to Be

So if repentance is foundational to the message of Jesus and the apostles, and if it brings forgiveness of sins and the gift of eternal life and escape from wrath, then what is it? And how does it relate to saving faith? It would seem that repentance is playing the role assigned to faith. Faith is how we receive the forgiveness of sins (Acts 10:43). Faith is how we have eternal life (John 6:47; 1 Tim. 1:16). Faith is how we escape condemnation (John 3:18; 2 Thess. 2:12).

I think many people see a bigger problem in the relationship between faith and repentance than is really there. They tend to see repentance as an outward turning from evil works. When viewed this way, there is a serious problem if repentance becomes the door to the forgiveness of sins (which it is). This view of repentance makes it sound as though we need to clean up our behavior as a means of attaining forgiveness and a right standing with God. But that would contradict the biblical teaching of justification by faith alone. And it would obscure the crucial truth that we clean up our behavior *because* we are forgiven in Christ, not *in order to* get into Christ and find forgiveness (see chapter 11).

Repentance Is the Reversal of What We Treasure

The problem with that view—that repentance is an outward turning from evil works—is that repentance in the New Testament does not refer to such an outward turning from evil works. Repentance refers to a deep, God-given change of heart that is almost synonymous with John's description of being born again (John 3:7; 1 John 5:1) and Paul's description of becoming new creatures in Christ (2 Cor. 4:6; 5:17; Eph. 2:10; 4:24).[2] Therefore, repentance is not competing with the role of faith in our salvation, any more than the new birth

---

2 Repentance is as much divine work and gift as is saving faith. We see this most clearly in 2 Tim. 2:24–26: "The Lord's servant must not be quarrelsome but kind to everyone, able to teach, patiently enduring evil, correcting his opponents with gentleness. *God may perhaps grant them repentance* leading to a knowledge of the truth, and they may come to their senses and escape from the snare of the devil, after being captured by him to do his will." We also see it in Acts 5:31: "God exalted [Jesus] at his right hand as Leader and Savior, *to give repentance to Israel* and forgiveness of sins"; and 11:18: "to the Gentiles also *God has granted repentance that leads to life.*"

does. Repentance is the miraculous transformation of our inner being so that its bent toward treasuring self-exaltation is replaced with a new bent toward treasuring God-exaltation.

We can see this if we make four observations from the New Testament.

1. The Word Metanoeō

First, the meaning of the Greek word behind the English *repent* (μετανοέω, *metanoeō*) does not refer to a change in behavior (though that follows, as we shall see). It has two parts: *meta* and *noeō*. The second part (*noeō*) refers to the acting of the mind, understood broadly so as to include not only its thoughts and perceptions but also its dispositions and purposes. In repentance the functions of mind and heart are not completely distinct, as we will see below when we discuss Acts 8:20–22. The first part (*meta-*) is a prefix that regularly means movement or change.[3] So the basic meaning of *repent* is to experience a change of the mind's perceptions and dispositions and purposes. One could say, without stretching the meaning, a change in what one treasures.

2. New Deeds Are Not the Repentance

Second, we can see that *repentance* does not refer to an outward change of behavior because the outward change of behavior is required as the *fruit* of repentance. It is called "fruits in keeping with repentance" (Luke 3:8). Paul summed up his ministry as the

---

3 For example, *meta* is used as a prefix in the word *metabainō* (transfer or change from one place to another), *metaballō* (change one's way of thinking), *metagō* (lead or move from one place to another), *metatithemi* (convey from one place to another, put in another place, transfer), *metamorphoō* (change in a manner visible to others, be transfigured), *metastrephō* (cause a change in state or condition, change, alter), *metaschematizō* (change the form of something, transform, change), etc.

pursuit of this: "[I] declared . . . to the Gentiles, that they should repent and turn to God, performing deeds *in keeping with their repentance*" (Acts 26:20). This turning is the heart's redirection from prizing this world to prizing God. This is repentance. And its effect is new behavior called "deeds in keeping with repentance" (ἄξια τῆς μετανοίας ἔργα πράσσοντας, *axia tēs metanoias erga prassontas*). The deeds are not the repentance. They are the fruit.

Similarly John the Baptist said to the crowds, "Who warned you to flee from the wrath to come? Bear fruits *in keeping with repentance*" (ποιήσατε οὖν καρποὺς ἀξίους τῆς μετανοίας, *poiēsante oun karpous axious tēs metanoias*, Luke 3:7–8). Then he gives examples of the fruits that are *in keeping with repentance*. To the crowds: "Whoever has two tunics is to share with him who has none, and whoever has food is to do likewise." To tax collectors: "Collect no more than you are authorized to do." To soldiers: "Do not extort money from anyone by threats or by false accusation, and be content with your wages" (Luke 3:11–14).

Repentance is not behavior change. It gives rise to behavior change. It is a change of mind and heart (*meta-noeō*). The command to repent is the command to experience an inner change that will lead to outer change. In the same way, the new birth and the new creation in Christ lead to outer change.

3. The Magician's Heart

Third, when Peter confronted Simon the magician with Simon's desire to buy the gift of God with money, he located Simon's wickedness in his *heart* and prescribed repentance as the remedy:

> May your silver perish with you, because you thought you could obtain the gift of God with money! You have neither part nor lot

in this matter, for *your heart* [καρδία, *kardia*] *is not right* before
God. *Repent*, therefore, of this wickedness of yours, and pray
to the Lord that, if possible, *the intent of your heart* [καρδίας,
kardias] may be forgiven you. (Acts 8:20–22)

Twice Peter says that Simon's problem is located in his heart. His
heart is not "straight" (εὐθεῖα, *eutheia*) toward God. Its "intent"
(ἐπίνοια, *epinoia*) needs to be forgiven. The heart is what changes
in repentance. It changes fundamentally toward God. Simon had
a love affair with power, magical power. He knew only worldly
ways of getting what he loved. He thought he could buy divine
power with money. What he needed was a whole new orientation
of his heart toward God. It was crooked in its orientation. It was
bent away from God toward self-exalting power. It needed to be,
as it were, straightened. Then the "intentions" of his heart would
be Godward. God-exaltation, not self-exaltation, would be his
treasure. That would be repentance.

4. Repentance toward the Glory of God

Fourth, in the book of Revelation, John speaks of unbelievers refusing to "repent of their deeds" (16:11), and "the works of their
hands" (9:20), and "their murders" (9:21), and their "sexual immo-
rality" (2:21). This emphasis on repenting from outward behaviors
does not contradict the point that repentance is the inner change of
the mind and heart. It simply assumes what we have said—namely,
that the inward change of the heart bears fruit in good outward
deeds; and the way to be done with evil outward deeds is to get a
new heart, that is, to repent.

One text in Revelation in particular is significant for the point
I am making. John says:

The fourth angel poured out his bowl on the sun, and it was allowed to scorch people with fire. They were scorched by the fierce heat, and they cursed the name of God who had power over these plagues. *They did not repent and give him glory.* (Rev. 16:8–9)

That last sentence is not translated literally. Literally it says, "They did not repent *to give him glory*" (οὐ μετενόησαν δοῦναι αὐτῷ δόξαν, *ou metenoēsan dounai auto doxan*). Giving God glory is not merely *added to* repentance, as though one does the one and then perhaps the other. No. Giving God glory is part of the very nature of what repentance does. That's the kind of change it is. It is the change of mind and heart (*metanoia*) from self-exaltation to God-exaltation.

Giving God glory describes the new "intent of [the] heart" (Acts 8:22) that Peter said Simon must experience in repentance. When Paul said to the Ephesian elders that while he lived with them he testified to Jews and Greeks of "*repentance toward God* and of faith in our Lord Jesus Christ" (Acts 20:21), this is what he had in mind most essentially. Every human being has a heart that by nature is "bent" (Acts 8:21, cf. εὐθεῖα, *eutheia*) away from loving the glory of God. We prefer created things (Rom. 1:23). A whole new orientation toward God must happen. This is what Paul means by "repentance *toward God*" (εἰς θεὸν μετάνοιαν, *eis theon metanoian*, Acts 20:21). John names the essence of that new orientation: repentance to give glory to God (Rev. 16:9).

Repentance and the Awakening of Faith

From these four observations, I conclude that repentance in the New Testament is not a change in outward behavior, but a change in heart and mind. It is virtually the same change that happens in the new birth (John 3:7) and the new creation in Christ (Eph. 2:10). In this change, the mind sees God differently and the heart treasures God differently. The eyes of the heart are opened to the glory of God in the face of Christ (2 Cor. 4:6). The heart is set free by this sight of the true beauty and worth of God in Christ. It is no longer in bondage to the deception that the fleeting pleasures of sin are superior to the treasures of Christ.

In repentance, therefore, the heart is unbent and made straight toward the glory of God. God in Christ becomes the heart's and the mind's supreme treasure. In this, God is glorified. The most natural thing in the world for such a new heart orientation is to experience saving faith in Jesus. This is why Paul summed up his message as "repentance toward God and . . . faith in our Lord Jesus Christ" (Acts 20:21). The awakening of repentance toward the supreme worth of the glory of God is simultaneous with the awakening of saving faith as the treasuring of Christ who is the image of God (2 Cor. 4:4).

In our evangelism, we call people to repentance toward God, and we call them to saving faith in Jesus. When we speak of *repentance*, we put the focus on the bent and sinful condition of our hearts. They must be changed. They must undergo repentance, *metanoia*. When we speak of *faith*, we put the focus on the positive experience of the heart that comes into being with repentance—namely, faith in Jesus. Repentance is the change of the mind and heart moving from unbelief to belief. From the pleasures of self-exaltation to the pleasures of God-exaltation. From false faiths to saving faith. From treasuring this world supremely to treasuring Christ above all.

25

Does Affectional Faith Make Evangelism Impossible?

WHEN I MAKE EXPLICIT the affectional nature of saving faith—namely, that it includes treasuring Christ above all—some people think that I have made evangelism harder, or even impossible.

To them, urging people to trust Christ, or to believe Christ, or to receive Christ seems more specific and clear and doable. It seems to them that in seeking to lead a person out of unbelief into faith, it is more likely that the new convert would be able to say, "I *trust* Christ as my Savior and Lord," than that he would be able to say, "I *treasure* Christ as my Savior and Lord."

Behind this concern is the sense that *trusting Christ* is a decision we can make and know we have made, while *treasuring Christ* is an affectional experience (like an emotion) that we can't *make* or *do*, and over which we don't have the same control. There is also the sense that an affection, like treasuring, involves degrees of greater or lesser intensity, earnestness, or sincerity, while trust is more black and white, either-or. You have it or you don't.

So there are two concerns here that I need to address. First, there is the concern that I have made evangelism virtually impossible, or at least much harder, by arguing that saving faith includes affectional elements like treasuring Christ. And, second, there is the concern that I have made faith variable and unstable, because affections always have differing degrees of intensity and sincerity. How would one ever know if one has saving faith if the heart's treasuring of Christ is so variable? The first concern seems to imperil evangelism. The second seems to imperil assurance. We will deal with these one at a time, in this chapter and the next.

You Make Decisions, but You Do Not Make Affections

Behind the concern about the impossibility of evangelism is the thought that people can't turn on and off their affections like they can their decisions. Decisions are doable. Affections are not doable in the same way. Affections are a kind of reflex in the mind and will from experiencing something. *Fear* arises if you hear someone breaking into your house in the middle of the night. *Joy* arises when you get news that your husband is coming home alive from the war. *Thankfulness* arises when the doctor says the cancer is gone. *Amazement* arises when you see an impossible triple backflip in an Olympic floor exercise. *Wonder* arises when you see the Milky Way in a cloudless sky at midnight from a mountain in Utah.

Spiritual affections are not identical with such heartfelt responses (as I explained in the introduction). But they are similar. The spiritual affections in saving faith are the special work of the Holy Spirit in response to spiritual perceptions of Christ. But they are responses of the heart, not just the mind, and so they share in the emotional life. They are more than decisions. So the concern applies to spiritual affections as well as to natural emotions.

The difference between affections and decisions is that with decisions you deliberate and consciously decide. You *make* decisions. You need not *feel* them. If you feel them, more is going on than a decision, though the feeling and the decision may be intertwined. It is true that we may be able to take steps to experience affections. We can decide to go to the places where wonder and amazement are likely. We can decide to go to a horror movie, where fear is likely to happen. We can study classical music until our appreciation turns into pleasure. But in the moment, when someone is calling for us to have saving faith, we can't will affections into being. We can't just choose to experience Christ as a treasure. Treasuring does not happen instantaneously merely by our choice.

None of this implies that spiritual affections are amoral. They are not like a fever or hiccups. When I suggest that they *happen* to us, I do not mean that they happen the way goosebumps happen. The perceiving *mind* and the inclining *will* are both involved in the kind of "happening" I have in mind. If an emotion happens to us with no connection to the mind and the volition, it has no moral standing. It is not morally good or evil.

I distinguish, for example, between the spiritual affection of the fear of God, on the one hand, and the physical sensation of sweaty palms or knocking knees, on the other. Those physical sensations are not what I mean by spiritual affections. We are not responsible to have sweaty palms. But we are responsible to have the fear of God, and all other godly affections that accord with the reality we confront. This is true even though those affections are not in our immediate control. They are gifts.

Sin Is the Culprit

My first response to this concern is that in the New Testament itself, saving faith is humanly impossible. I have not made it impossible. Sin has made it impossible. When the rich young man turned away from Jesus and refused to follow him (Matt. 19:22), Jesus said it is easier for a camel to go through the eye of a needle than for the rich to enter the kingdom of heaven (Matt. 19:24). The disciples were astonished and said, "Who then can be saved?" And Jesus responded, "With man this is *impossible*, but with God all things are possible" (Matt. 19:25–26).

Paul underscored this condition of the natural human heart with the words, "The natural person does not accept the things of the Spirit of God, for they are folly to him, and *he is not able to understand them* because they are spiritually discerned" (1 Cor. 2:14). And again, "The mind of the flesh [= the natural mind] is hostile to God, for it does not submit to God's law; indeed, *it cannot*" (Rom. 8:7, my translation). Or again, "We were *dead* in our trespasses" (Eph. 2:5). And that deadness included *blindness* to the glory of Christ: "The god of this world has blinded the minds of the unbelievers, to *keep them from seeing* the light of the gospel of the glory of Christ, who is the image of God" (2 Cor. 4:4).

Reversing the Concern

So I would reverse the direction of this concern that I am responding to. Instead of being concerned that I have made saving faith impossible, we ought to be concerned that so many are trying to make it possible. Instead of being concerned that I have put saving faith beyond the powers of the natural man, we ought to be concerned that so many are adjusting the meaning of faith so that it is within the powers of the natural man. That's the real danger in our modern age. The kind of decision that the natural man finds doable without the miracle of new birth is not a saving decision. Judas *decided* to follow Jesus, and he wasn't saved. I discussed in chapter 2 how the cultural air we breathe encourages us to treat faith as a humanly manageable act.

God Does the Humanly Impossible through Humans

How then does evangelism proceed in the pursuit of the humanly impossible? It proceeds with this conviction: through the preaching of Christ, God performs the miracle of new birth, giving rise to saving faith. Through the sharing of the gospel over coffee in a café, the Holy Spirit miraculously turns that sharing into a divine showing of the glory of Christ.[1] Paul said that Christ sent him (and us!) to do the humanly impossible. "I am sending you to open their eyes, so that they may turn from darkness to light and from the power of Satan to God" (Acts 26:17–18).

The people Paul was sent to evangelize were blind to the light of Christ (2 Cor. 4:4). They were dead in trespasses and sins (Eph. 2:1–3). They were in bondage to Satan (2 Tim. 2:26). But Paul is sent to open their eyes and to give them life and freedom. So are we. We are sent to give sight to the blind and life to the dead. We are sent to do the impossible. The impossible happens in our evangelism because God gives liberty and life and sight when his Son is put on display in the gospel. Lydia is a case in point. Paul spoke the gospel, and "the Lord opened her heart to pay attention to what was said by Paul" (Acts 16:14). Paul did not open her heart.

---

1   I recorded an episode of the *Ask Pastor John* podcast on how to lead someone to Christ that I thought might be helpful to mention here: "How Do I Lead Someone to Christ?," August 10, 2020, Desiring God website, https://www.desiringgod.org/.

God did—through the word of the gospel. God did the humanly impossible through a human.

Evangelism is indispensable in saving sinners. "I planted, Apollos watered, but God gave the growth" (1 Cor. 3:6). Humans plant; humans water. God does the impossible. He gives life. Between the blindness of 2 Corinthians 4:4 and the miracle of God-given sight in 2 Corinthians 4:6 is the indispensable verse 5—Paul's proclamation of Christ: "What we proclaim is not ourselves, but Jesus Christ as Lord, with ourselves as your servants for Jesus' sake." That was the means of the miracle of verse 6: "God . . . has shone in our hearts to give the light of the knowledge of the glory of God in the face of Jesus Christ."

Dry Bones, Hear the Word of the Lord!

Paul wasn't the first person sent to do the impossible. God stood Ezekiel before a field of dry bones and said, "Prophesy over these bones, and say to them, O dry bones, hear the word of the LORD" (Ezek. 37:4). That is what all evangelism is—speaking the word of God over dry bones. So why is it not hopeless? Because God said, "Behold, I will cause breath to enter you, and you shall live. And I will lay sinews upon you, and will cause flesh to come upon you, and cover you with skin, and put breath in you, and you shall live, and you shall know that I am the LORD" (Ezek. 37:5–6).

The Call Creates the Life

Another way to see the human role in the impossibility of evangelism is to notice that God turns our gospel invitation into an act of creation. When Jesus stood before the tomb of Lazarus, it would have been right to say that it is humanly impossible for that dead man to walk out of the tomb. And it would be humanly foolish to talk to him and ridiculous to tell him to come out. But Jesus "cried out with a loud voice, 'Lazarus, come out.' The man who had died came out" (John 11:43–44). The call created the life.

So it is with our evangelism. God makes human words work miracles. He causes the dead to live, the blind to see, and the deaf to hear. They hear the voice of Jesus. "My sheep hear my voice, and I know them, and they follow me" (John 10:27). We don't know who his sheep are. Our job is to make the message of Christ known. God's job is to give his sheep ears to hear. They already belong to him, chosen before the foundation of the world (Eph. 1:4). They are already his (John 17:9). When the gospel is preached, he gives them life and sight and ears to hear and faith: "As many as were appointed to eternal life believed" (Acts 13:48). We plant. We water. We evangelize. God gives life and faith.

Presenting Christ as True *and* Precious

The affectional dimension of saving faith—the treasuring of Christ above all—does not make faith humanly impossible. Sin has already done that. But seeing saving faith this way *does* have an effect on our evangelism. If you are persuaded that saving faith not only involves believing in Christ as true, but also involves treasuring Christ as precious, then you will strive in your evangelism not only to reason with people and persuade their minds that Christ is true (Acts 17:2, 17; 18:4, 19; 19:8; 24:25), but also to describe the greatness and the beauty and worth of Christ. You will present him from your mind to their minds as completely true, and from your heart to their hearts as supremely valuable.

You will include in your accolades of Jesus not only his inestimable gifts of forgiveness and justification and eternal life, but also his unsearchable glory as a person. You will strive not to allow the gospel presentation to become prudential—that is, merely expedient. You will not speak as though Christ were simply *useful* in attaining all a person ever wanted in his sinful condition. Instead, you will try to show with Scripture, and with your own experience, that there are wonders and pleasures in relation to Christ that are better than the best pleasures of earth. You will seek to show that Christ, in and beyond all his gifts, is a pleasure to be with—forever.

We Show Jesus, God Surprises with Joy

We cannot make wonder and astonishment and admiration happen in a person's heart. But God can. And he does it by opening people's spiritual eyes (Eph. 1:18) to what we show them in the word of God. We can't make them see Christ as their supreme treasure. But we can point to the treasure with joy and do our best to describe the treasure and its effect in our lives. Our job is to show. God's job is to surprise with joy.

How do we show the treasure? We go to the Bible and fill up our treasure chest with the glories of Christ. We meditate on them. We are transformed in our affections by them (2 Cor. 3:18). And as God gives opportunity, we open the chest and bring out the treasures for people to see. Here's a partial collection of Christ's glories from my treasure chest:[2]

- the treasure of his *deity*, equal with God the Father in all his attributes—the radiance of his glory and the exact imprint of his nature, infinite, boundless in all his excellencies;

2 I brought out a version of this collection first at a conference in 2004: "Sex and the Supremacy of Christ, Part 2," Desiring God 2004 National Conference, https://www.desiringgod.org/.

- the treasure of his *eternality* that makes the mind of man explode with the unsearchable thought that Christ never had a beginning but simply always was—sheer, absolute reality while all the universe is fragile, contingent, like a shadow by comparison to his all-defining, ever-existing substance;

- the treasure of his never-changing *constancy* in all his virtues and all his character and all his commitments—the same yesterday, today, and forever;

- the treasure of his *knowledge*, which makes the Library of Congress look like a matchbox, and all the information on the Internet look like a little 1940s farmer's almanac, and quantum physics seem like a first-grade reader;

- the treasure of his *wisdom* that has never been perplexed by any complication, and can never be counseled by the wisest of men;

- the treasure of his *authority* over heaven and earth and hell— without whose permission no man and no demon can move one inch; who changes times and seasons, removes kings and sets up kings; who "does according to his will among the host of heaven and among the inhabitants of the earth; [so] none can stay his hand or say to him, 'What have you done?'" (Dan. 4:35);

- the treasure of his *providence*, without which not a bird falls to the ground or a single hair of any head turns black or white;

- the treasure of his *word*, which moment by moment upholds the universe, and holds in being all the molecules and atoms and subatomic worlds we have never yet dreamed of;

- the treasure of his *power* to walk on water, cleanse lepers, heal the lame, open the eyes of the blind, cause the deaf to hear and storms to cease and the dead to rise, with a single word, or even a thought;

- the treasure of his *purity* never to sin, or to have one millisecond of a bad attitude or an evil thought;

- the treasure of his *trustworthiness* never to break his word or let one promise fall to the ground;

- the treasure of his *justice* to render in due time all moral accounts in the universe settled, either on the cross or in hell;

- the treasure of his *patience* to endure our dullness decade after decade, and to hold back his final judgment on this land and on the world, that many might repent;

- the treasure of his sovereign, yet submissive, *obedience* to keep his Father's commandments perfectly and then embrace the excruciating pain of the cross willingly;

- the treasure of his *meekness* and lowliness and tenderness that will not break a bruised reed or quench a smoldering wick;

- the treasure of his *wrath* that will one day explode against this world with such fierceness that people will call out for the rocks and the mountains to crush them rather than face the wrath of the Lamb;

- the treasure of his *grace* that gives life to spiritually dead rebels, and awakens faith in hell-bound haters of God, and justifies the ungodly with his own righteousness;

- the treasure of his *love* that willingly dies for us even while we were sinners and frees us for the ever-increasing joy of making much of him forever;

- the treasure of his own inexhaustible *gladness* in the fellowship of the Trinity, the infinite power and energy that gave rise to all the universe and will one day be the inheritance of every struggling saint.

And this collection of treasures is but a taste (1 Pet. 2:3). Time would fail to speak of the treasures of his severity, and invincibility, and dignity, and simplicity, and complexity, and resoluteness, and calmness, and depth, and courage. If there is anything admirable, if there is anything worthy of praise anywhere in the universe, it is summed up supremely in Jesus Christ.

"He is the radiance of the glory of God and the exact imprint of his nature, and he upholds the universe by the word of his power. After making purification for sins, he sat down at the right hand of the Majesty on high" (Heb. 1:3). That is where he is today as you read this book. That is where he is as you share the gospel. And by his Spirit, while on his throne, he is with you. He will help you.

He will uphold you. He will give you what you need to say (Isa. 41:10; Matt. 28:20; Luke 12:11–12).

I am not making evangelism impossible. Sin did that. I am trying to make it biblical, bold, hopeful, and lavish with the treasures of Christ. My prayer is that, for all this, it will be more fruitful "for the sake of his name among all the nations" (Rom. 1:5).

26

Does Affectional Faith
Undermine Assurance?

THE CONCERN IN THIS chapter is that the affectional nature of saving faith makes faith variable and unstable, because affections always have differing degrees of intensity or earnestness or sincerity. How would one ever know if one has saving faith if the heart's treasuring of Christ can be so variable?

I Did Not Create This Problem

My first response to this is to say that I am not the one who has made faith variable and subject to many degrees. The Bible itself shows that faith is variable and subject to change.

- Faith can increase and grow. "Our hope is that as your *faith increases*, our area of influence among you may be greatly enlarged" (2 Cor. 10:15). "The apostles said to the Lord, 'Increase our faith!'" (Luke 17:5). "Your faith is growing abundantly" (2 Thess. 1:3).

- Faith can be great or little. "O woman, great is your faith!" (Matt. 15:28; 8:10). "O you of little faith" (Matt. 6:30; see Luke 17:6).

- Faith can be weak or strong. "[Abraham] did not weaken in faith" (Rom. 4:19; 14:1). "He grew strong in his faith" (Rom. 4:20; cf. Acts 16:5).

- The faith of God's elect can fail temporarily but not utterly. "I have prayed for you [Peter] that your faith may not fail. And when you have turned again, strengthen your brothers" (Luke 22:32). Then he denied the Lord three times (Luke 22:54–62). But then, in answer to Jesus's prayer, he repented!

- Faith can exist alongside some measures of unbelief. "I believe; help my unbelief!" (Mark 9:24).

As Jonathan Edwards wrote, "Among those who have a spiritual sight of the divine glory of the gospel, there is a great variety of degrees of strength of faith, as there is a vast variety of the degrees of clearness of views of this glory."[1]

I Ask Every Christian

I would ask those who raise this concern: Do you, with your different view, never deal with weakening faith? Do you never have greater or lesser confidence in the promises of God? Do you never have doubts enter your mind that the Bible is true or that you are an authentic Christian? Are there no days or hours when

---

1   Jonathan Edwards, *Religious Affections*, ed. John E. Smith and Harry S. Stout, rev. ed., vol. 2, *The Works of Jonathan Edwards* (New Haven, CT: Yale University Press, 2009), 306–7.

the deceitfulness of indwelling sin gets the upper hand and you do what you hate instead of trusting God to deliver you? Do you think that the faith you had at the point of your conversion meets no assaults on the way to heaven, and does not need to be stirred up with varying strength to fight for perseverance?

And as you "fight the good fight of the faith" and seek to "take hold of the eternal life" (1 Tim. 6:12), do you never wonder if you have fought well enough? When James tells you that good deeds of love are the sign that faith is alive and real (James 2:17, 26), do you never wonder, "Have I done enough of those deeds of love?" When Hebrews tells you to "strive for . . . the holiness without which no one will see the Lord" (Heb. 12:14), does the variableness of your holiness never make you wonder if it is sufficient to confirm your faith? When Paul tells you, "If you live according to the flesh you will die, but if by the Spirit you put to death the deeds of the body, you will live" (Rom. 8:13), do you never struggle with whether you have sincerely put your sins to death like that?

Is it really because I have treated saving faith as affectional that our hearts are troubled with the variableness of our faith and holiness? Do you really have a view of faith that puts you above these struggles? Do you really have a kind of faith to offer unbelievers that will spare them the lifelong fight of faith?

Where Does Cavalier Confidence Come From?

My experience is that people who go about their Christian lives with a casual inattention to the fight of faith—who are not "diligent to confirm [their] calling and election" (2 Pet. 1:10), who do not "strive for . . . the holiness without which no one will see the Lord" (Heb. 12:14), who do not give thought to Jesus's statement that "the one who endures to the end will be saved" (Mark 13:13), or to Jesus's words "Be faithful unto death, and I will give you the crown of life" (Rev. 2:10)—such careless people, I have found, are mistaken not mainly in their view of saving faith but in their view of eternal security.

They have the superficial and unbiblical notion that "once saved, always saved" means that there is no earnest warfare in salvation. For them, conversion to Christ is like a vaccination against the damning effects of sin. They got the vaccination, so now they can breathe in the virus of sin year after year and feel secure against hell. They can break out with sinful sores all over, and never see them as the prelude to hell. They got the vaccination.

But that is not what the Bible teaches about eternal security. To be sure, God's elect will be saved, and nothing can stop him from saving them. He predestined them for eternal sonship (Eph. 1:5), and he will have them for himself forever. "Those whom he predestined he also called, and those whom he called he also justified, and those whom he justified he also glorified" (Rom. 8:30). None falls out between justification and glorification. They are secure. Nothing can separate them from the love of Christ (Rom. 8:38–39).

But, oh, how naive and unbiblical it is to think that conversion is like a vaccination. Conversion is like a terminally ill cancer patient being introduced to an amazing physician who has the only cure in the world. His cure is not a vaccination. It is a lifelong treatment of moment-by-moment protection from the guilt and power of the cancer of sin, in fellowship with the doctor. The protection is not chemo. It is not radiation. It is a satisfying friendship with the doctor. The doctor is the medicine. This great physician only admits patients whom he intends to heal. He is omnipotent and cannot be thwarted in his intentions. To be converted is to discover his amazing kindness and faithfulness and power and saving skill.

But this lifelong treatment engages the mind and heart of the patients. No one drifts away from the doctor and lives. No one puts the doctor out of mind and lives. No one ignores the doctor's instructions and lives. No one presumes that past years of treatment are sufficient, and leaves the doctor, and still lives. The doctor doesn't save his patients by saying the treatment and the friendship don't matter. He saves them by restoring to them again and again the joy of his fellowship and the glad confidence that his painful therapy will bring them to heaven.

Evangelism Is Not the Offer of a Vaccination against Damnation

In our evangelism, we do not offer vaccinations against damnation. We offer Christ. We offer the Great Physician. We offer a living relationship of daily fellowship with the only person in the world who can save. We offer a life of spiritual warfare with sin and Satan and the world. We offer salvation by faith—but an embattled faith. A faith ever under attack. A faith, therefore, that has countless degrees of strength and weakness. Not just from season to season or day to day, but from hour to hour. Which of us who have known the Lord Jesus for any length of time does not know that the measure of joyful confidence we have after a sweet walk through the word at 7:00 a.m. will become a fading, half-hearted assurance by noon, and a holding on by our fingernails by dusk?

Neither in evangelism nor in our own lives do we hide the fight of faith. We are not calling people to leave the battlefield, but to enter it. What we offer them is a triumphant, all-satisfying Christ, a band of fellow warriors, an indwelling Spirit of victory, an infallible manual of guidance, and irrevocable divine promises of help and preservation. "He who began a good work in you will bring it to completion at the day of Jesus Christ" (Phil. 1:6). "May your whole spirit and soul and body be kept blameless at the coming of our Lord Jesus Christ. He who calls you is faithful; he will surely do it (1 Thess. 5:23–24). "[He] is able to keep you" (Jude 1:24). He promises, "I will never leave you nor forsake you" (Heb. 13:5); "I am with you always, to the end of the age" (Matt. 28:20).

God Keeps Us Saved, and Makes Us Sure

What then of the question, How would one ever know if one has saving faith, if the heart's treasuring of Christ can be so variable? I hope we have seen that this question of assurance is not unique to my understanding of saving faith. It is shared by all of us. All true Christians experience the variableness of faith. All of us wonder from time to time if we are truly the children of God. This battle to believe and to maintain full assurance is not new and was already there in the New Testament.

Paul told the Colossians that he wanted them to "reach all the riches of full assurance of understanding and the knowledge of God's mystery, which is Christ" (Col. 2:2). The writer to the Hebrews expressed a similar desire: "We desire each one of you to show the same earnestness to have the full assurance of hope until the end" (Heb. 6:11). The apostles knew that all of us need divine help in being sure that we are the children of God. We cannot maintain our faith or our assurance without God's daily, omnipotent sustaining grace. Only God can keep us faithful, and only God can make us sure that we are saved.

Paul's Path to Assurance

Paul gave us the most pointed promise in this regard:

If you live according to the flesh you will die, but if by the Spirit you put to death the deeds of the body, you will live. For *all who are led by the Spirit of God are sons of God.* For you did not receive the spirit of slavery to fall back into fear, but *you have received the Spirit of adoption* as sons, by whom we cry, "Abba! Father!" The *Spirit himself bears witness with our spirit that we are children of God.* (Rom. 8:13–16)

What is plain from this text is that God wants his children to enjoy the assurance that they really are in his eternal family. He does not want us to languish in uncertainty or be paralyzed in our ministry by nagging questions about the authenticity of our faith. Paul gives two paths to assurance.

One is in 8:14: "All who are led by the Spirit of God are sons of God." In the immediate context, being "led" refers to being led into the great work of sin-killing—the killing of our own sin, by the Spirit. Verse 13: "If by the Spirit you put to death the deeds of the body, you will live. *For* all who are led by the Spirit of God are sons of God." The connection between verses 13 and 14 shows that the "leading" of the Spirit in verse 14 supports the killing of sin in verse 13. In other words, when we hate our own sin and make war on it by the Spirit, we experience compelling, God-given evidence that we are the children of God.

The other path to assurance that Paul mentions is the authentic cry of childlike, glad-hearted dependence on God as our Father. This cry, welling up authentically from within, is the Spirit's witness in us that we are God's children. "We cry, 'Abba! Father!' The Spirit himself bears witness with our spirit that we are children of God." This is similar to what Paul said in 1 Corinthians 12:3: "No one can say 'Jesus is Lord' except in the Holy Spirit." That is, no one can authentically, from the heart, cry out with sincere glad-hearted submission, "Jesus is the Lord of my life!" unless the Spirit is bearing that witness within him.

The Spirit Assures Us

These are the paths of assurance that we are the children of God. First, we see that the Spirit is at work in our lives, leading us to hate our sin, and make war on it, and put it to death. Second, we see that the Spirit is at work in us to arouse us, from deep in our hearts, to cry with childlike affection, "God is my all-supplying Father!" Third, we see that the Spirit is at work in us to cause our hearts to call out with authentic, glad submission, "Jesus is my sovereign, my captain, my pilot, my Lord!"

Along these three paths, as well as others revealed in Scripture, the Spirit assures us that

- our estimation of the truth and greatness and beauty and worth of Christ is real—Christ is indeed supremely valuable, over all the world;

- our heart's embrace of Christ as supremely satisfying is authentic;

- our enjoyment of Christ's gifts, natural and spiritual, is not idolatry but rather a genuine taste of God himself, with a glad overflow of thanksgiving;

- our old self, which still tastes the pleasures of sin, died with Christ, and its remaining desires are breathing their last and do not come from our true self—the new creation in Christ;

• and our failures to delight in Christ more than in sin is hated by our true selves, and our warfare against sin is real opposition rather than resigned complicity.

This is the gift God gives to his children. He has "sealed [us] with the promised Holy Spirit, who is the guarantee of our inheritance until we acquire possession of it, to the praise of his glory" (Eph. 1:13–14). With this *seal* and *guarantee* and *witness* of the Spirit, the affectional dimensions of saving faith, while never perfect in this life, are sustained and confirmed for our peace and courage in the service of love.

Conclusion

Saving Faith, Designed for the Glory of God

MOST OF MY WRITING and preaching for the past fifty years has consisted of arguments, explanations, applications, and celebrations relating to the astounding truth that *God is most glorified in us when we are most satisfied in him*. This book is no exception.

That God would design saving faith to include affectional dimensions, which I have summed up in the phrase *treasuring Christ*, is no surprise. For in this way, he built God-glorifying pleasure into the Christian life from beginning to end. It is there from the first millisecond of new life in Christ, for it is there in saving faith. Not perfect, not without variation, not unassailed, but real. And it will be there forever because in God's presence is fullness of joy and at his right hand are pleasures forevermore (Ps. 16:11).

Abraham Grew Strong in His Faith, Giving Glory to God

John Owen does not say things carelessly. So we should be slow to discount his remarkable statement that "the essence of faith consists in a due ascription of glory to God."[1] He was meditating on Romans 4:20, where Paul considers Abraham's faith:

> No unbelief made [Abraham] waver concerning the promise of God, but *he grew strong in his faith, giving glory to God* [ἐνεδυνα-μώθη τῇ πίστει, δοὺς δόξαν τῷ θεῷ, *enedunamōthē tē pistei, dous doxan tō theō*], fully convinced that God was able to do what he had promised. (My translation)

What Owen saw in Paul's words was that faith is of such a nature that when a person experiences it, God is glorified in him. The most obvious way to express this is to say that when a sinner has unwavering faith in God's promise, though all human odds are against it, that faith makes God look gracious, powerful, and trustworthy. Which is to say, faith glorifies God. "[Abraham] grew strong in his faith, [thus!] giving glory to God."

Trusting God to Be Our Great Reward

What I have tried to do in this book is press into the nature of such God-glorifying faith. The fact that we have found saving faith to have affectional dimensions that embrace Christ as a treasure shows even more clearly and fully how faith glorifies God.

Paul was not unaware that Abraham trusted God not only to give him a miracle-born son and a great tract of land, but also to be for him a satisfying reward—to be his portion, his inheritance. In Genesis 15:1, the Lord said to Abram, "Fear not, Abram, I am your shield, *your very great reward* [אָנֹכִי מָגֵן לָךְ שְׂכָרְךָ הַרְבֵּה מְאֹד, *anōkiy magen lak shecarka harbēh me'od*]" (my translation). Yes, this last

---

1 John Owen, *The Glory of Christ*, vol. 1, *The Works of John Owen*, ed. William H. Goold (Edinburgh: T&T Clark, n.d.), 295.

phrase can be translated, "Your reward will be very great." But that would leave open the question, What is the great reward?

God's greatest promise to Abraham gives the answer: "I will establish my covenant between me and you and your offspring after you throughout their generations for an everlasting covenant, *to be God to you* [לִהְיוֹת לְךָ לֵאלֹהִים, *liheyōt leka leʾlōhim*] and to your offspring after you" (Gen. 17:7). Whatever else Abraham's reward was, this was the greatest—the promise, the reality that "I will be with you as your God. I will be God to you. I myself am your greatest reward."

Having God himself as our treasure was the apex of faith among the Old Testament saints. "My flesh and my heart may fail, but God is the strength of my heart and *my portion* forever" (Ps. 73:26). "I cry to you, O LORD; I say, 'You are my refuge, *my portion* in the land of the living'" (Ps. 142:5). "'The LORD is *my portion*,' says my soul, 'therefore I will hope in him'" (Lam. 3:24). Of course, the Lord gave many gifts, not least of which were a miracle-born son and the promised land. But the greatest gift, the greatest reward, the greatest promise was "I will be God to you." I, God, will be yours. Your portion. Your great reward.

Confirming His Contentment in God

Abraham showed by his life that God was his portion. He avoided strife with his kinsman Lot by letting him choose any portion of the land. Lot took the best (Gen. 13:9–11). Abraham was content. God was his portion. Abraham even pleaded to God to spare Sodom and Lot's family (Gen. 18:23). Abraham gave Melchizedek a tithe of all the booty he recovered in saving his family (Gen. 14:20). Abraham refused the booty offered by the king of Sodom (Gen. 14:22–24). We are meant to see that God himself was Abraham's great reward.

Therefore, Abraham's faith gave glory to God not only because it displayed God's grace and power and trustworthiness, but also because that grace and power and trustworthiness, and all else that God is, were Abraham's portion. His greatest reward. His supreme treasure.

A Trusted God Is Glorified, a Treasured God Is More Glorified

God is glorified when he is trusted as true and reliable. He is more glorified when this trust is a treasuring trust—a being satisfied in God as our great reward. Or, as we would say on this side of the incarnation of Christ, a being satisfied with all that God is for us in Jesus. God designed saving faith as a treasuring faith because a God who is treasured for *who he is* is more glorified than a God who is only trusted *for what he does*, or *what he gives*. When God himself is treasured as the reward, he is more glorified than when he is only trusted as the rewarder. This is the ultimate reason for what we have seen in this book, and why I wrote it.

God's Aim to Be Outwardly Glorified

But this ultimate reason—that God be most glorified in a kind of faith that is most satisfied in him—is still more expansive and all-inclusive. The glorification of God by the invisible acts of the human soul is too limited. Faith—the trusting and treasuring of all that God is for us in Jesus—is an act of the soul, not the body. It is essentially invisible to mortals. We cannot see another person's heart. But God did not create the universe to be glorified only in regions that he alone can see.

Thus, the day is coming when "the righteous will shine like the sun in the kingdom of their Father" (Matt. 13:43). That righteousness will be a great part of our brightness. To be sure, our glorified bodies will be part of our brightness, to the glory of God. Our present bodies are "sown in dishonor" but "raised in glory" (1 Cor. 15:43). But the Christ-exalting glory of the saints in the age to come will not mainly be the brightness of our immortal bodies. It will mainly be the beauty of our sinless souls whose holy thoughts and purposes and affections will be manifest in the perfections of inward *and outward* holiness.

Christ did not die to have an inwardly pure but outwardly plain bride. "Christ loved the church and gave himself up for her, that he might sanctify her . . . so that he might present the church to himself in splendor, without spot or wrinkle or any such thing, that she might be holy and without blemish" (Eph. 5:25–27). God meant, from the beginning, that his Son would have a holy and pure and spectacularly beautiful bride forever. He intended that his people would be "filled with the fruit of righteousness that comes through Jesus Christ, to the glory and praise of God" (Phil. 1:11). He meant our righteousness to be visible to the world for his own glory, as Jesus said: "Let your light shine before others, so that they may see your good works and give glory to your Father who is in heaven" (Matt. 5:16).

I tried to show in chapter 11 that saving faith is the root of all this God-glorifying transformation. Paul explained that God is the one who fulfills every "*work of faith*" by his power, so that the name of *our Lord Jesus may be glorified*" (2 Thess. 1:11–12). All our holiness, now and forever, is a "work *of faith.*" Our outward righteousness comes from an inward treasuring trust in a great Savior. This faith is designed by God as a treasuring trust so that "our Lord Jesus may be glorified."

The Christ-Exalting Key to the Beauty of Holiness

Thus, God accomplished two God-glorifying purposes in design-ing saving faith as an affectional act—as a treasuring trust. First, a

Savior who is treasured for his all-satisfying worth is more glorified than a Savior who is only trusted for his competence.

Second, in designing saving faith as a miraculous, God-given treasuring of Christ above all, God made this faith the key to breaking the power of sin and bearing the fruit of righteousness. That is, God designed the invisible act of trusting and treasuring Christ in such a way that it would be the power to produce visible righteousness and love.

Saving faith, as it receives Christ, trusting and treasuring all that God is for us in him, is the way God unites us to Christ. In this union, God is 100 percent for us forever. He will never cast us out (John 6:37; 10:28–29). We are justified permanently (Rom. 8:30). And the very same instrument by which God unites us to Christ—namely, saving faith—also severs the root of sin. The root of sin is the treasuring of other things above God. Saving faith is the God-given treasuring of Christ above all. Therefore, saving faith severs the root of sin. It does so by a positive force—the preference for Christ and all his ways. By the miraculous new birth, Christ becomes our joy. And this joy overflows in righteousness and love (Luke 14:14; 2 Cor. 8:2; Heb. 10:34; 12:2).[2]

Therefore, saving faith is designed by God, not only as an inward, invisible act of treasuring Christ, but also as an act that bears visible, God-glorifying fruit in bodily behavior. It is precisely the nature of saving faith as a treasuring trust that gives it the power that severs the root of sin and bears the God-glorifying fruit of visible righteousness and love. This is the beautification of Christ's

---

2 In *Future Grace: The Purifying Power of the Promises of God* (Colorado Springs, CO: Multnomah, 2012), I have tried to spell out in great detail and practical application how faith, as being satisfied with all that God is for us in Christ, actually transforms and purifies the bride of Christ. A shorter version of *Future Grace* was published as *Battling Unbelief: Defeating Sin with Superior Pleasure* (Colorado Springs, CO: Multnomah, 2007).

bride. She will treasure him above all, and everything she does will reflect his worth. This will be the beauty of her holiness. She will be most satisfied in him, and thus he will be most glorified in her.

Treasuring Christ Never Ceases

Saving faith will never cease. Oh, yes, some of its powers will no longer be needed in the age to come. "Now we see in a mirror dimly, but then face to face" (1 Cor. 13:12). In that sense, sight replaces faith (2 Cor. 5:7). Nor will we have any sin to put to death. Faith, as the great severing axe on the root of sin, will be hung on the wall of heaven as a glad memorial of God's keeping and sanctifying power.

But, oh, the trusting and treasuring reality of saving faith! That will never cease. "Now faith, hope, and love *abide*" (1 Cor. 13:13). Saving faith abides. It remains forever. We will forever depend utterly on God. Through Jesus Christ, we will trust him for every moment's existence and for every good gift of the new creation.

But we will not trust him merely as a competent sustainer of the universe, nor merely as an inexhaustible giver of created gifts. We will trust him as an all-satisfying, never-ending treasure. We will welcome him moment by moment forever as our supreme and inexhaustible pleasure. Saving faith will have reached its goal—the perfections of Christ and all that God is for us in him, glorified by our being satisfied in him forever.

END

Appendix

A Response and Challenge

THE MOST SERIOUS CRITICISM that my book has received from advance reviews is that I teach "justification by love," not justification by faith alone. I have tried to make the book clearer and more compelling since reading those reviews. I hope the book as it stands (especially chapters 3 and 4) is clear enough and true enough to persuade most readers that this serious criticism is not valid. But I will offer one more affirmation and clarification, along with a challenge.

An Affirmation

It is wrong to say we are justified by love rather than by faith alone. Faith alone is the instrument by which the Holy Spirit unites us to Christ, whose blood and righteousness are alone the ground of God's becoming 100 percent for us (justification). Nor is trusting Christ identical with loving Christ. One cannot replace faith with love as if they were interchangeable.

A Clarification

So where does the criticism come from?

What causes the misunderstanding is that I press into saving faith by asking, What is it? Or, What are we doing when we believe on Christ? My answer is that saving faith is essentially a *receiving* of Christ (John 1:11–12). We must have Christ in order to be justified and finally saved, because Christ alone bore our sins and became our justifying righteousness. Nothing in us is seen or reckoned as our justifying righteousness—not faith in any of its dimensions, nor any of its fruits. Christ alone is the ground of God's becoming forever 100 percent for us.

Faith is the instrument chosen by God for uniting us to Christ for this justification, because faith is "peculiarly a *receiving* grace" (to use again the phrase from Andrew Fuller). It justifies not because it merits God's acceptance, but because it receives Christ. He alone is the ground of our coming into an eternal right standing with God.

Then I press in further and ask, When this saving faith receives Christ, what does it receive Christ *as*? Saving faith receives Christ *as what*? I ask this because *receive* by itself is a neutral act implying nothing about whether what we are receiving is excellent or only expedient—enjoyed for itself, or useful only for getting something you enjoy more. I answer that saving faith receives Christ as valuable, precious, satisfying—a treasure. Thus, saving faith is a treasuring receiving, a treasuring believing, a treasuring trust, a treasuring faith.

When I see "treasuring Christ" as an element of saving faith, I am not leaving behind the truth that faith is "peculiarly a *receiving* grace." For *treasuring*, as an aspect of faith, is also a peculiarly *receiving* grace—a receiving act of the soul. It is not a "*giving* grace."

This is absolutely crucial to see, because one of my critics observed that I am replacing the "receiving grace" of faith with a "giving grace" like treasuring. But treasuring Christ, as I am using the phrase, is emphatically not a *giving* grace but a *receiving* one. It offers nothing. It wants everything. It no more gives to Christ than thirsty lips give to the cup of living water. Drinking with satisfaction is not giving. It is receiving. Treasuring is "peculiarly a *receiving* grace."

Then I use other words to describe this aspect of saving faith called *treasuring* Christ. I use words and phrases like *delighting in, being satisfied with, enjoying,* and *loving*—all having Christ as their object. As I use these terms, all of them are receiving graces, not giving graces. They are not performances. They are the reflexes of emptiness looking away to Christ.

This is the context for understanding the meaning and role of *love to Christ* in this book. It is another name for treasuring Christ. Therefore, like treasuring, it is not *in addition to,* nor *the result of,* trusting Christ. It is an aspect of trusting Christ. It is another name for treasuring, and therefore it has the same role as treasuring.

A Challenge

Let me shift from a defensive posture to an offensive one. I share with my critics the Protestant and Reformed zeal to magnify the majesty and glory and all-sufficiency of God in Christ. My heart leaps with joy when I read how Calvin exalted the glory of God as the main issue of the Reformation. He wrote to his Roman Catholic adversary Cardinal Sadolet, "[Your] zeal for heavenly life [is] a zeal which keeps a man entirely devoted to himself, and does not, even by one expression, arouse him to *sanctify the name of God.*" This was Calvin's chief contention with Rome's theology: it does not honor the majesty of the glory of God in salvation the way it should. He goes on to say to Sadolet that what is needed in all our doctrine and life is to "set before [man], as the prime motive of his existence, *zeal to illustrate the glory of God*."[1]

I believe this profoundly biblical impulse is what motivates my critics when they say, for example, "At stake is the 'alien' character of Christ's righteousness, the very divide with Rome." In other words, the glory of Christ will be diminished if we intrude our own righteousness into the glorious and all-sufficient work of Christ as the sole ground of our justification. To which I say, with all my heart, Amen! Let us be willing to die for this. As many have.

But now, as I go on the offensive, the stakes are raised. The ultimate issue is the glory of Christ. We agree. How, then, is Christ glorified by saving faith? For surely this is why God decreed that faith would be the instrument of justification—because faith would glorify God better than any other way of our being united to Christ (Rom. 4:20). How, then, does saving faith glorify Christ in the divine act of justification?

My critics and I would gladly agree that faith glorifies God in justification because it is divinely suited, as a *receiving* grace, to call all attention to Christ. Saving faith glorifies Christ by looking away from self to Christ alone—to his all-sufficiency, including his alien righteousness, without which we could have no right standing with God. In this, we all agree and shout for joy.

But it gets even better. There is more glory to give to Christ as we receive him for justification. To be sure, the glory of Christ is at stake in protecting his righteousness from any intrusion of our own righteousness, compromising the sufficiency of his. Amen! Let the glory of Christ blaze in the all-sufficiency of his alien righteousness, as the only ground of our acceptance with God.

---

1   John Calvin, *John Calvin: Selections from His Writings*, ed. John Dillenberger (Missoula, MT: Scholars Press, 1975), 89.

But there is more glory to break out into view because of God's design for faith alone to unite us to Christ. What is at stake is not only the *sufficiency* of Christ's work, but also the *worth* of it, the *beauty* of it, the all-satisfying *glory* of it. Or to be more accurate, what is at stake in the way we are justified is the shining forth of the worth of *Christ* himself, the beauty of *Christ*, the glory of *Christ* reflected in the justifying faith of his people.

In other words, God ordained for faith to be the instrument of justification not only to magnify the *sufficiency* of Christ's alien righteousness, but also to magnify its *infinite beauty and worth*. Faith is not an expedient acceptance of an all-sufficient achievement that I use to escape hell and gain a happy, healthy, Christless heaven. God did not design faith as the instrument of justification in order to turn the alien righteousness of Christ into a ticket from self-treasuring misery in hell to self-treasuring pleasure in heaven.

No. God designed faith as the instrument of justification precisely to prevent such utilitarian uses of the work of Christ. This is why saving faith is not only the acceptance of Christ as all-sufficient, but also the embrace of Christ as our treasure. Faith perceives and receives Christ—the sole ground of our justification—not only as efficacious, but as glorious. Not only as sufficient, but as satisfying.

Therefore, my challenge to all who share a zeal for the all-sufficiency and glory of Christ in the work of justification is this: do not preserve the power of faith to glorify the sufficiency of Christ's work by stripping faith of its power to glorify his all-satisfying worth.

When I define *love* to Christ as *treasuring* the glory of Christ in his all-sufficiency, including the sufficiency of his alien righteousness, I do not turn justification by faith into justification by keeping the moral law. On the contrary, I insist that God, in his word, has appointed faith alone as the instrument of justification because it glorifies Christ's righteousness not only as useful but also as precious. It does so because, as a treasuring grace, it magnifies his all-satisfying worth.

General Index

Abraham, grew in faith, 273–76
acts of faith, 62n9
adoption, 222
affectional faith, and self-determination, 36–37
affections, 49; natural and spiritual, 14; and saving faith, 13
allegiance, faith as, 74, 75–78
anxiety, 96–97
assensus (assent), 18, 58, 65, 194
assurance, 22, 27, 113–15, 216, 268–71
author intention, 89

bare assent, 40, 45, 48, 54
Bates, Matthew, 75–85
Bavinck, Herman, 58, 131–32n2
beholding glory, 157–59
belief, 17
believing: as coming to Christ, 206–7; as receiving Christ, 44, 101–2, 198; and satisfaction in Christ, 202–3; as spiritual drinking and eating, 199–201
believing the truth, 181, 188
believing in vain, 26, 141, 239
Bible, infallibility of, 73
boasting, 130
Boice, James, 31
boredom, 157

"born of God," 44
by faith, 168–70

Calvin, John: on justification by faith, 40; on pious affection, 60–61; reply to Sadolet, 283–84; on saving faith, 11
Carey, William, 49
Chafer, Lewis Sperry, 31
Christian Hedonism, 22
Christian life, hardships of, 169
coming to Christ, 206–9
commandments of God, not burdensome, 190, 193
compassion, in evangelism, 223
confidence, 114, 176; in evangelism, 223
confidence in the flesh, 149, 151
contentment in God, 275
"contrary to doubt," 95–96
conversion, not like a vaccination, 266
cost of discipleship, 216, 229–34
Council of Trent, 41, 42, 43, 83
cross-bearing, 231, 233

dead faith, 140–41
deception, and failure of faith, 186
decisions, and affections, 216, 252–53
"decisions" for Christ, 37
delight, 34n11
delight in Christ, 72–73

Scripture Index

⁙ desiringGod

Everyone wants to be happy. Our website was born and built for happiness. We want people everywhere to understand and embrace the truth that *God is most glorified in us when we are most satisfied in him*. We've collected more than thirty years of John Piper's speaking and writing, including translations into more than forty languages. We also provide a daily stream of new written, audio, and video resources to help you find truth, purpose, and satisfaction that never end. And it's all available free of charge, thanks to the generosity of people who've been blessed by the ministry.

If you want more resources for true happiness, or if you want to learn more about our work at Desiring God, we invite you to visit us at desiringGod.org.

desiringGod.org